What Every Therapist
Needs to Know
about Treating Eating
and Weight Issues

A Norton Professional Book

What Every Therapist Needs to Know about Treating Eating and Weight Issues

Karen R. Koenig

W. W. Norton & Company

New York · London

For information about permission to reproduce
selections from this book, write to Permissions,
W. W. Norton & Company, Inc.
500 Fifth Avenue, New York, NY 10110

For information about special discounts for bulk
purchases, please contact W. W. Norton Special Sales at
specialsales@wwnorton.com or 800-233-4830

Manufacturing by Courier Westford
Book design by Carol Desnoes
Production manager: Devon Zahn

Library of Congress Cataloging-in-Publication Data

Koenig, Karen R., 1947–
What every therapist needs to know about treating
eating and weight issues / Karen R. Koenig. — 1st ed.
p. ; cm.
"A Norton professional book."
Includes bibliographical references and index.
ISBN 978-0-393-70558-4 (pbk.)
1. Eating disorders—Treatment. 2. Obesity—Treatment.
3. Lifestyles—Health aspects. 4. Food habits—Psychological
aspects. I. Title.
[DNLM: 1. Eating Disorders—therapy. 2. Feeding
Behavior—psychology. 3. Appetite. 4. Body Image.
5. Overweight—therapy. 6. Psychotherapy—methods.
WM 175 K78w 2008]
RC552.E18K643 2008
616.85'26—dc22

                                        2008019438

W. W. Norton & Company, Inc.
500 Fifth Avenue, New York, N.Y. 10110
www.wwnorton.com

W. W. Norton & Company Ltd., Castle House
75/76 Wells Street, London W1T 3QT

1 2 3 4 5 6 7 8 9 0

*To all the researchers
in the field of eating disorders,
thanks for setting the record straight
about food and weight.*

Contents

Acknowledgments

First thanks goes to Deborah Malmud, director of the Professional Books Division of W.W. Norton & Company, Inc., who thought I might be the right person to write a book describing how eating and weight issues weave their way through psychotherapy. I hope I have put to paper what she had in mind. Appreciation also goes to Vani Kannan, editorial assistant, and Kristen Holt-Browning, assistant managing editor, for their help. Special thanks goes to Nancy L. Cloak, MD, of Sheppard-Pratt Hospital in Towson, Maryland, for making sure I got my medical facts right. Once again, my agent, Janice M. Pieroni of Story Arts Management has been there with unflagging encouragement every step of the way.

Preface

Every year there are copious books written for the general public about dieting and weight loss. Usually there are also a number of books devoted to educating therapists on the treatment of conditions such as anorexia and bulimia nervosa. Many are geared to the clinician who is already treating clients with these serious conditions and who specializes in eating disorders.

But what about the generalist who treats a wide range of complaints and rarely (if ever) has a client with anorexia or bulimia? What of the clinician whose clients occasionally gripe about their weight or hint at over- or undereating without flagging these issues as a major concern? What of the practitioner who needs help recognizing clients' concerns about food as they arise throughout the stages of life? What about the therapist who recognizes that her client is struggling with serious eating and weight issues, but does not know how to approach or treat them?

This book is written to help practitioners who do not specialize in eating disorders recognize and treat the major and minor food and weight problems they encounter in their practice. By major, I mean those problems that have plagued a client throughout life and substantially affect functioning—sociability, interpersonal relationships, self-esteem, fitness, health, and the ability to create a happy and meaningful life. Major problems include a lifetime of food restriction or binge eating, maintaining a weight that is dangerously high or low, frequently yo-yoing between extreme weights, suffering from malnutrition, or believing that one is not thin enough when the mirror tells a different story. Minor problems are those that are transitory and less serious, such as minimal weight gain after pregnancy, adjusting to hormonal changes that show up on the scale, weight gain or loss due to medication, carrying around 5 to 10 extra pounds that simply will not come off and stay off, or ignorance about proper nutrition that can be resolved through education.

This book is based on the assumption that over the course of a career, the average practitioner may have taken a college elective course or a couple of professional development workshops on eating disorders, and may even have read journal articles or a book on the subject. However, it assumes that the clinician does not consider herself an expert, may be uncomfortable assessing and treating eating and weight problems, or may simply be ignorant about how concerns about food and body size play out in life and weave their way through psychotherapy.

It is highly likely that therapists will come across clients that struggle with food or weight at some point; according to the Web site of the Multi-service Eating Disorder Association, Inc. (MEDA), 66% of adult Americans are considered overweight or obese, 50% of women define themselves as overweight (even when they are not!), 80% of adults have dieted during their lifetime, and 60 million Americans are trying to lose weight ("General Eating Disorder Fact Sheet," MEDA Web site). Although clients may turn up on our doorstep worried about depression, frightened by escalating marital conflict, feeling overwhelmed, or wanting a new career, many of them will have subclinical food problems that need to be addressed. Even highly skilled clinicians, of course, are not expected to know every client issue right off the bat, and food problems might not be on our radar. However, given the numbers above, it pays to keep an open mind and expect that some clients will bring us their struggles with eating and weight, along with their other problems.

My interest in this field is both professional and personal. As a therapist and educator, I have been working with people who have food issues for 30 years and have authored numerous articles on eating and body image dysfunction for clinicians and the general public. I have written two books—*The Rules of "Normal" Eating: A Commonsense Approach for Dieters, Overeaters, Undereaters, Emotional Eaters, and Everyone in Between!* and *The Food and Feelings Workbook: A Full Course Meal on Emotional Health.* From the start of my career, my mission has been to teach people with eating problems how to eat "normally"—that is, to provide them with the skills that "normal" eaters use instinctively and automatically every day to take pleasure in food and maintain a comfortable weight for life.

Toward this end, I have taught "Quit Fighting with Food" workshops in the communities in which I have worked, and trained colleagues in professional development programs in the cognitive-behavioral treatment (CBT) model I use and favor. I have lectured to social workers, psychologists, registered dieticians, fitness instructors, medical students, and other professionals in the health and mental health fields. More and more, my experience has led me to recognize that most people—and that includes seasoned clinicians—do not understand the complicated and multifaceted root causes of food and weight problems and therefore have difficulty addressing them with clients.

On a personal level, I began struggling with food in my teens and continued through my early 30s—alternating between dieting and overeating—until I discovered the concept of intuitive eating. With both curiosity and trepidation, I began to read about disordered (often called dysfunctional) eating, gradually stopped dieting, and eventually gave up bingeing as well. I entered therapy with a general therapist who, fortunately, was able to help me overcome my food abuse problems. After my own success, I worked in a Massachusetts-based program teaching people how to make peace with food.

This book came about after Deborah Malmud, director of the Professional Books Division of W. W. Norton and Company, Inc., read an article I wrote for *Social Work Today* on what I call "the rules of 'normal' eating" and my therapeutic approach. She wondered if I might be interested in writing a book for therapists on the subject, and I jumped at the chance. More than my two previous books, *What Every Therapist Needs to Know about Treating Eating and Weight Issues* pulls together all my experience—as a disordered eater, client in treatment, and therapist—to help practitioners treat two of the major issues of our time, eating and weight.

What Every Therapist
Needs to Know
about Treating Eating
and Weight Issues

Introduction

There was once a time when the solution to excess weight was singular and simple: just go on a diet, we were told. Take in fewer calories and watch the pounds slip away. This recourse developed from the long-held view that overeating is a moral issue—consume in moderation, exert some self-control, and all will be well.

As science began to understand and explain that being overweight was far more of a physical problem than a moral failure, we learned that, along with ingesting fewer calories, we needed to expend more energy to burn them off. Before long, however, another factor emerged in the equation. We discovered that it mattered not only how much we ate, but what and when—small, frequent meals accelerated calorie burn-off, carbohydrates and proteins each affected appetite differently, and metabolism was more complex than anyone could have imagined.

Further studies went on to conclude that all appetites are not created equal and that hormones, heredity, and biochemistry play a far greater role in eating and weight regulation than we previously thought. We learned that specific foods alter our biochemistry and moods and that genetics may largely predetermine weight and body structure. We found out that appetite hormones and neurotransmitters were a major determinant of whether we could easily control our appetite and lose weight (not to mention regulate emotions!), and that medication and surgery could be utilized to reach our weight and eating goals.

No matter how complicated the issue of eating and weight became, however, our solution remained more or less the same—eat less and exercise more. It is easy to see how this cookie-cutter model stuck with us. Let's face it, it is difficult for anyone not trained as a neurobiologist to understand the complexities, subtleties, and far-reaching implications of weight management. Moreover, because the subject has become so complex, it is easier to think in terms of moderation and self-discipline, which are simple and familiar concepts that have been reinforced for centuries, than to bone up on the latest weight-loss study results.

At the same time that science was redoubling its efforts to discover the causes and treatments for obesity, serious problems began to crop up at the other end of the eating spectrum, namely, an increase in cases of anorexia and bulimia nervosa. For decades these conditions were viewed as rare and somewhat exotic. Now it is hard to remember a time when they were not in our clinical lexicon. Although health practitioners (and society) learned quickly to recognize the gravity of anorexia and bulimia, it took time to develop theories about causes and efficacious treatments. Initially, the roots of these disorders were thought to be solely psychological and intrapsychic. In time, psychology began to view them as being caused, or at least exacerbated, by family dynamics, traumatic events, and societal pressures to be thin. Now we have discovered that, like overeating, anorexia and bulimia are strongly influenced by biological factors. Anorexia is not merely rebellion against parents in the service of separation and individuation; bulimia is not a symbolic rejection of the internalized bad mother.

So, where does all this rapidly changing information leave the average, conscientious therapist who tries to keep up with the latest developments in many fields—depression, anxiety, attention deficit/hyperactivity disorder (ADHD), trauma, addictions, child development, and personality disorders, among others? How can she best serve clients who have eating and weight problems without receiving extra training in the field of eating disorders or returning to school to earn a PhD in neuroscience? How can she make accurate assessments to pick up and focus on the minor as well as major eating and weight concerns of the men and women she serves? The answers lay ahead in the pages of this book.

In spite of the fact that being overweight has a strong physiological component, talk therapy is extremely successful in helping clients resolve eating and weight issues. Treatment can be integrated into any specialty—couples or family, brief treatment or psychoanalysis, solution-focused or eye movement desensitization reprocessing (EMDR)—and may be addressed in a variety of therapeutic models—cognitive-behavioral, relational, dialectical behavioral, Gestalt, and sensorimotor, to name a few.

It makes sense that medically trained clinicians such as psychiatric nurses might want to use their science training to help clients understand the biology of eating and weight management, while strict behaviorists might lean more toward helping clients set up a successful system of rewards and incentives to reach their goals. Whatever our discipline or expertise, we can use talk therapy to help clients move toward identifying, understanding, and resolving their eating issues.

Another aspect of how we view and interpret eating and weight issues is dependent on our own or our intimates' struggles with them. If we have had—or continue to have—problems, will it make us more or less empathic with a client who eats or weighs too much or too little? How may the success or failure of our attempts to resolve our own food problems affect our willingness and ability to talk about a client's relationship with food and her body, and the way that weight impacts health, self-esteem, and relationships?

It is time that we start to view food and weight problems not as separate from the rest of our clients' issues, but as integrated into them. Although not every client has eating concerns that are central to therapy, many have an unhealthy relationship with food and their body, which impacts and impinges on nearly every aspect of life. Just as no competent therapist believes that sexual abuse, marital difficulties, or addictions are self-contained, no therapist should treat eating and weight issues per se as irrelevant or inconsequential to a client's overall mental (and physical) health.

Most clients with eating and/or weight problems arrive at my office after decades of struggling with food and the scale. Chronic overeaters or undereaters or, more often, yo-yoers between the two, they are at the end of their rope and run the gamut between expecting miracles and fearing that they are beyond help. Aware of my experience in the eating disorder field, many expect that I will recognize what is wrong with them immediately and know exactly how to fix them. I often do have an inkling about the causes of their food dilemmas and tentative assumptions about how to get their eating back on track, but I certainly do not have all the answers.

According to MEDA, considering that at any given time in this country 45% of women and 25% of men are on a diet, two things are clear ("General Eating Disorder Fact Sheet," MEDA Web site). The first is that a significant portion of our population is concerned about losing weight, and the second is that they consider dieting the way to do it. Not surprising! There are some 17,000 diet methods and plans available, and the diet industry spends between $40 billion and $50 billion annually to promote them ("General Eating Disorder Fact Sheet," MEDA Web site). Dieting is so acceptable that people who want to shed pounds do not think twice about giving the South Beach or Atkins diet a whirl and cannot imagine any other way to take it all off. From magazines to medicine, we are led to believe that diets work.

But do they? One statistic that has remained steady throughout the 3 decades I have worked in this field strongly challenges conventional wisdom about dieting: 95% of people who diet and lose weight regain it, and 90% regain more than they originally lost. Meta studies of diets across the board keep coming up with this same conclusion: only 5% of dieters keep the weight off for more than 5 years ("General Eating Disorder Fact Sheet," MEDA Web site). When we think of it that way, how many of us would throw everything we have into an investment that, at the outset, offers such a paltry chance for success? Moreover, a survey of more than 30 studies on dieting and weight loss found that "the benefits of dieting are simply too small and the potential harms of dieting are too large for it to be recommended as a safe and effective treatment for obesity" (Guthman, 2008, p. 46).

Additionally, in my experience, people in that paltry 5% of successful dieters are often what I call "white knucklers," whose chief goal in life is to stay thin. They live in perpetual struggle with sugar and fat and most white foods and focus most of their energy on counting calories and rigid portion control. Moreover, when a segment of this group falls off the wagon, they often fall far. From never eating forbidden foods, they go to overconsuming them and, hence, put on all the weight they lost—35, 60, or even 100-plus pounds. So, while it is true that for some people diets do work, these superachievers pay a heavy price through deprivation and living in constant fear of food and fat.

Diets do not work for permanent weight loss, but that does not mean that people who are heavy need to be resigned to their weight. Many folks find healthy ways to keep weight off and have a positive, enjoyable relationship with food. With patience, practice, and perseverance, they learn, to a greater or lesser extent, the skills that "normal" or intuitive eaters (I use the terms interchangeably) employ instinctively and automatically to feel comfortable around food and maintain a healthy weight for life. "Normal" eating is called intuitive because it means making food choices based on body sensations, not external influences. "Normal" is in quotes because it does not describe one type of eater. It does, however, entail following a set of four rules: eating when hungry, making satisfying food choices, eating with awareness and enjoyment, and stopping when full or satisfied.

"Normal" eating was first advocated in the 1970s as the anti- or nondiet approach to weight loss. Unfortunately, in spite of consistent research proving that diets tend to make people fatter by decreasing metabolism and causing deprivation and rebound eating, intuitive eating has never won over large audiences. The process of change through intuitive eating is too difficult, too slow, and too demanding. And diets? They are simplistic, give us right-and-wrong instructions for success, and, unlike intuitive eating, do not require that we trust the bodies that got us into trouble in the first place. Diets are symptomatic of the superficiality of our culture and the appeal of magical thinking, our desire to cut corners, and our primitive wish to get something for nothing.

However, diets can be dangerous. Besides promoting undereating and causing rebound feeding, eating disorder experts consider them the gateway to serious problems with food. Thirty-five percent of dieters move on to yo-yo dieting and one-quarter of those who diet develop clinical eating disorders (Guthman, 2008). Naturally, not everyone who diets ends up engaged in pathological dieting, that is, restricting food in such a way that the practice becomes an obsession and causes health problems. However, a preoccupation with thinness may set the stage for a lifetime of food restriction and deprivation that permanently alters metabolism and is as destructive to a person's emotional health as any addiction.

One of the major problems with referring clients to diet plans and programs is that they are based on the faulty assumption that anyone who tries can succeed at losing weight and that failure to do so is due to lack of motivation and willpower. In short, diet failures blame the victim, which, as therapists, we work hard to avoid doing (think incest and physical abuse). Moreover, because they are simplistic, diets fly in the face of what every clinician knows and tries to teach clients—

that there are complex roots to most of our issues, that change takes substantial time and effort, that creating a life that is joyful and meaningful is not a linear process, that resolving our difficulties generally involves making changes in many, if not all, aspects of our lives, and that long-lasting transformation requires that we pay attention to who we are and want to be pretty much around the clock.

This book will help the reader gain confidence and competence in assessing and treating weight and eating issues through:

- understanding their multifaceted causes, providing a solid foundation for assessment approaches and treatment options, and giving a deeper appreciation of how strongly these issues may affect and permeate clients' lives;
- sorting out the non-life-threatening problems clients have with eating and weight from serious issues that undermine their physical and mental health and endanger their lives;
- identifying when food and body struggles may be symptomatic of more serious issues of mood problems, cognitive distortions, and impulse control disorders;
- recognizing and dealing with transference and countertransference issues that arise in therapy around size and weight issues between clinician and client.

Chapter One, "A Comprehensive Approach to Treating Eating, Weight, and Body Image Issues," lays out both the obvious and subtle ways that food disturbances intrude into a client's life and how to begin thinking like an eating disorders therapist. This chapter provides a context for making connections about assessing and addressing eating and weight issues with a wide range of clients. Chapter Two, "How Clients Express Themselves Through Food," looks at historical and cultural stereotypes of being fat, being thin, and overeating, offering an overview of how clients with eating and weight problems may perceive themselves and how others may see them. It describes the ways that disordered eating—along the continuum from minor to major dysfunction—may be a symbol of unspoken or unmet needs and how they get acted out with food and weight.

Chapter 3, "The Biology of Eating and Weight," is an explanation of the complexity of this subject matter due to variances in individual biochemistry, and how biochemical imbalances that lead to eating and weight problems also correlate to mood and impulse disorders. This chapter, more than any other, illustrates why diets fail to work for most people. Chapter 4, "Health and Medical Problems," provides a comprehensive description of what can happen when the body receives too little nourishment, and describes the physical consequences of being over- or underweight. Written in lay terms, it details how eating too many of the wrong foods and not enough of the right ones may lead to life-threatening health issues.

Chapter 5, "Personality Traits and Family Dynamics," offers an overview of the impact that personality has on eating problems and vice versa. It presents a context for understanding how characterological and family influences contribute to struggles with food and weight. Chapter 6, "Assessment," sets out the practitioner mind-set that is necessary for ongoing evaluation of subclinical food and body issues and provides tools for determining the nature and extent of motivation, dysfunction, and skills for recovery. The focus is on how clients might present with eating problems in therapy and how to relate them to other issues in their lives.

Chapter 7, "Clinical Disorders," explains how depressive, anxiety, and dissociative disorders relate to food and weight problems, as well as how trauma and sexual abuse can impact body image and the regulation of appetite. This chapter details how eating may be a way of coping with psychological problems as well as an activity that exacerbates them. Chapter 8, "Life-Cycle Issues," shows how eating and weight problems surface in various phases of life. It covers age-related stages as well as conditions such as pregnancy, menopause, and illness.

Chapter 9, "Nutrition and Fitness," explores what clinicians need to know to help clients eat healthily and become fit. It outlines the information that clients must have to nourish themselves adequately and achieve all-around fitness goals. In Chapter 10, "Transference and Countertransference," discussion turns to how unconscious biases of both clinician and client impact treatment of eating and weight issues. This chapter explores ways to anticipate how these processes may arise in treatment and how to deal with them if they do. Chapter 11, "Treatment Options," covers the numerous ways that therapists might address food and body struggles through material that clients bring up. This chapter also covers treatment traps that can bog down the therapy and prevent clients from finding solutions to eating and weight problems.

Each chapter contains two types of questions: those that encourage the therapist to reflect on therapeutic issues arising from the material being presented, and those that should be directed at the client to gain and clarify information, assess its relevance to treatment, and collaborate in moving forward. Questions for clients may be used as is or as a basis for exploring their responses.

This book is not meant to provide all the answers to treating people with eating and weight issues. Even experts in the field do not have them and need to rely on updated information about appetite and weight regulation, new scientific data about treatment options, experience and intuition, and consultation and supervision for difficult cases. If this book succeeds in increasing your clinical comfort and skill at assessing and treating weight and eating issues, it will have done its job.

CHAPTER 1

A Comprehensive Approach to Treating Eating, Weight, and Body Image Issues

As therapists, we may naturally assume that when clients enter our office, our goal is to care for their minds. Of course, we are actually treating their entire being. The Western mind-body dichotomy is not only a confusing, unhelpful paradigm for viewing clients, but also invalid. There is no mind separate from body, no body distinct from mind. On our deepest level we are a stew of chemicals that circulate throughout our cells, from the brain's amygdala to the minuscule muscles in our toes.

Nowhere is this mind-body integration more important than in assessing and treating weight and eating issues, for what we think and how we feel about the size, shape, appearance, functioning, and condition of our body is a result of both physical and psychological factors. Moreover, it is precisely this mind-body connection that is often functioning ineffectively. Our job is to help clients tease out what is fixed by nature from what is changeable, especially to help them transform irrational, unhealthy thinking to that which is sound and beneficial. Guiding clients to generate new, constructive thinking will in turn alter how they feel about physical aspects of themselves, even when those aspects are relatively immutable.

Unless and until something goes wrong, we may not think very much about our body or its parts. We may focus on our physical self when we are feeling particularly attractive or when we are relieved by the absence of physical pain. But some people with eating and weight issues think about their bodies far too often in some ways and not often enough in others. They awaken with the same drudge of a body they had when they fell asleep the night before, and start each day with the same dread of food and frustrations about what to wear. Some avoid mirrors, having given up on what they look like. Others jump on the scale the minute they rise to see whether the day will be a good or bad one, depending upon where the needle points. They then spend the rest of the day in an internal tug-of-war over meal choices, food deprivation, or a constant battle with appetite. Or they tune out body signals of hunger, cravings, enjoyment, and fullness and eat compulsively, impulsively, mindlessly—or not at all.

Sitting in a session, they may well put food difficulties on the back burner while focusing on other life issues—marriage, job, parents, children, managing a crisis, chronic pain or terminal illness, aging, or some life-changing decision looming before them. Because there is so much else to work on or because a critical issue needs immediate attention, they might touch on topics such as self-esteem and self-worth, but never mention how little or much they ate or how they spent the day obsessing about food. They may share health concerns, but avoid disclosing their incessant yearning to trade in their body for another, their terror at gaining even a pound, or the way their body hatred overshadows every other positive aspect of themselves.

Clients may not share these concerns for several reasons. Therapy sessions are time limited and clients often feel they barely have enough minutes to talk about crucial concerns. They know they have to prioritize what is most important and work on therapeutic goals that have been established. They may be so overwhelmed with difficulties that food and a number on the scale fall to the bottom of a towering heap of troubles. Crisis may be so much the norm that difficulties with eating or weight seem trivial or superficial. They may wish to focus on issues they think they can do something about—changing partners or careers, caring for children or elderly parents, or building interpersonal skills and relationships.

Lastly, these issues often exist under their radar, and clients may not realize how much stress they feel about their size or their eating. As with other ongoing discomforts or discontents, they simply get used to having them and fail to identify them as worth addressing, purposely avoid raising them because they fear they will be ignored or invalidated, or accept them because they do not believe they can be helped.

Alternately, for some clients, a nagging desire to lose that last 10 pounds, slim down after pregnancy, or regain appetite after chemotherapy may seem too petty to raise. They may think, *Gee, I really should go on a diet,* but it does not occur to them to ask for help in reaching eating, nutritional, or weight goals in a psychotherapist's office. They may not realize that any subject is—or certainly should be—fair game, especially if it prevents or minimizes good feelings about the self.

In order to understand what it feels like to be a person with an eating or weight issue, we first have to understand the range of problems or conditions we may encounter with clients. We have to recognize the special and significant role that food and weight play in today's culture and how that role defines the lives of the majority of Americans and, therefore, our caseloads.

Reflections for Therapist

1. In general, how have you viewed and treated client eating and weight concerns?
2. What are your assumptions about these issues?

3. When a client brings up food or eating issues, how do
    you usually feel? Respond?

4. Is talking about food and weight a comfortable issue for
    you? If not, why not?

5. How much do you know about eating disorders and prob-
    lems? Enough to treat them adequately? What do you
    need to learn to become a more effective clinician in
    these areas?

Just when we began to get used to the term *eating disorders* and
educating ourselves about anorexia and bulimia nervosa, along came a
new phrase, "disordered eating," which describes a way of thinking
and behaving around food that may not reach a level of clinical disorder but, nevertheless, is dysfunctional and benefits from treatment. In
talking about disordered eating, I am referring to a continuum—from
chronic dieting and fear of food and weight gain to the most severe,
life-threatening cases of anorexia, from compulsive and emotional
food consumption that causes gradual weight gain to binge eating,
which leaves a person exhausted and ill.

Most of us are familiar with the general description of anorexia
and bulimia nervosa, from which some 11 million Americans suffer
("Statistics," National Eating Disorders Association Web site).
Anorexia is diagnosed when a person refuses to maintain a minimal
weight that is conducive to health and well-being. Bulimia describes
a person who engages in binge eating, followed by self-harming com-
pensatory methods to prevent weight gain. Bulimia, in the form of
purging, laxative abuse, or excessive exercise, may also accompany
anorexia, such as when someone who has barely eaten believes she
has consumed too much and feels a need to ward off every ounce.

Binge eating occurs when a person eats well beyond the point of being full at least two times a week. It may be accompanied by bulimia, but more often is not. Additionally, it may occur alternately with anorexia; that is, a person may refuse to eat at a minimally healthy level for months or years at a time and remain dangerously thin, then turn around and eat so much so often that her weight balloons up. Binge eating also can be a rebound response to chronic dieting and rigid food deprivation that does not meet criteria for anorexia. This happens when a person severely restricts food intake, say, during the week, then "pigs out" over the weekend and resumes dieting Monday morning.

Rather than think of eating disorders as fixed, it is helpful to consider a more elastic mind-set. For example, people with bulimia may be thin/underweight or of normal weight, just as binge eaters may be obese, overweight, thin/underweight, or of normal weight. The number of pounds someone weighs and their size are insufficient indicators of whether or not they have eating problems; this can only be established by examining specific patterns of behavior over time.

Ranging along a continuum, some eating problems are easier to spot than others. Moreover, not everyone who appears to have an eating disorder warrants a bona fide clinical diagnosis. Obviously, a person of average height who tips the scale at 350 pounds is carrying excess pounds, if only because their heft may negatively affect their health. The problem may be due to eating, hormones, biochemistry, lack of exercise, genetics, or any mix of factors. Alternately, someone who is 5′6″ and barely weighs 85 pounds is likely to suffer from anorexia, but their low weight could as easily be due to serious medical conditions such as end-stage cancer, untreated celiac disease or Crohn's disease, or AIDS. Moreover, even though we may assume that someone who is overweight eats too much, overeating may not be their problem. Instead, they may be ignorant about nutrition and eat fairly "normally" but unhealthily; that is, they may not consume too much food but an excess of foods that are high in calories and fat.

There are also people we cannot identify through appearance as having eating problems who chronically diet or undereat and who binge or overeat (or alternate between the two extremes of behavior in a day, week, or month), but maintain a normal weight. These clients often carry the diagnosis of eating disorder "not otherwise specified" (NOS) and tend to slip through the clinical cracks. Although the diagnosis is common in outpatient settings and can be severe and long-standing, it is not always taken seriously because it does not meet criteria for anorexia, bulimia, or binge eating disorder.

An unusual type of eating disorder that affects about 1.5% of the population and may be difficult to diagnose, sleep eating disorder, is characterized by abnormal eating patterns during the night, including uncontrolled eating urges and splurges—generally of high-sugar, high-fat foods—that clients do not remember when they awaken. According to the Sleep Disorders Guide Web site, symptoms include having little or no appetite for breakfast, consuming more food during the night than during a meal, weight gain, daytime fatigue, and unexplained bruises from sleepwalking. Low levels of melatonin and cortisol, fluctuating hormones, sleep apnea, restless-leg syndrome, and/or stress all may be factors causing sleep eating disorder ("Sleep Eating Disorders," Sleep Disorders Guide Web site).

To assess whether the client has anorexia, bulimia, binge eating disorder, compulsive/emotional eating, or sleep eating disorder, ask:

1. How would you describe your relationship with food?
2. Have you ever been diagnosed with an eating disorder? Which one? When? Did you receive treatment? When? Where? For how long?
3. Have you ever thought you might have an eating problem?

4. Have you resolved your eating problems (completely, incompletely, not at all)?

5. How do you feel about your body and your weight now? In the past?

6. Do you regularly do any of the following: avoid food even when you are very hungry, eat past full or when you are definitely not hungry, vomit or use laxatives after eating, feel you must compensate for eating/overeating by exercising, awaken in the middle of the night and eat large quantities of food, have questions about what is enough with food, believe that you are too fat or too thin although weight charts and everyone else says you are at a healthy weight?

Is there one kind of client who is most likely to have eating and weight problems—older women, adolescents, whites or blacks, people from certain cultures, those who are anxious or depressed, folks who have addictions, those who have suffered significant trauma? No one age range or diagnosis captures the market, although the more difficulty people have regulating affect and behavior, the more likely they may be to over- or underdo with food.

Certainly any woman raised in contemporary America is at risk for eating and weight problems. In fact, I know of an eating disorder therapist who is writing a book based on the premise that *every* woman in this country cannot help but have some kind of eating problem. While that may or may not be true, it is safe to assume that being raised in our fat-phobic, thin-obsessed culture makes it difficult, if not impossible, for women to be satisfied with their bodies and more than likely that they will want to slim down to fit a cultural ideal.

The female American body "ideal" is tall, long-boned and long-legged, slim-hipped, flat-bellied, and medium- to large-breasted with good muscle tone. It is okay to be petite, but better to be tall so that—insist fashion designers—clothes will hang better on the female form. These days it is becoming more acceptable for a woman to be muscular, but not so much so that it might detract from her femininity. With an increased medical and media focus on fitness over the past few decades, men, too, are succumbing to the desire for a long, lean look and washboard abs. The "ideal" man is tall, broad-shouldered, and well-muscled.

Eighty percent of American women are dissatisfied with their appearance ("Statistics," National Eating Disorders Association Web site). An *ELLEgirl* poll found that 30% of 10,000 readers would rather be thin than healthy (Martin, 2008). According to the National Eating Disorders Association Web site, only one woman in 40,000 has the current ideal body size and shape, which translates numerically into 5′9″ tall and 110 pounds. Instead, the average American woman is 5′4″ tall, weighs 140 pounds, and wears a size 14 dress. In fact, most fashion models are thinner than 98% of American women and only 7% of us are model material (tall, long-boned, and angular!) ("Statisitics," National Eating Disorders Association Web site). No wonder 90% of us are so unhappy with our bodies that we believe we need to lose weight ("General Eating Disorder Fact Sheet," MEDA Web site). It is vital to remember that there is actually nothing verifiably better about this ideal, and that many people are aspiring to a standard that is not only dangerous, but impossible to reach.

Most statistics of men with eating disorders are accepted as an underestimation because men may be more ashamed than women to report their symptoms to health care professionals. Women report feeling almost twice as guilty about the food they eat as men, which may account for the fact that 45% of American women and only 25% of men are on a diet on any given day ("Statistics," Anorexia Nervosa and Related Eating Disorders Web site).

Binge eating disorder affects some 3.5% of American women and

2% of men, but is likely considerably underdiagnosed in part because it has only recently been the recipient of substantial research and media attention, and in part because many people may consider themselves overeaters, emotional eaters, or even compulsive eaters without defining themselves as having binge eating disorder (Szep, 2007). Moreover, cultural factors may affect our perception of the amount we eat because some ethnic groups do not consider overeating problematic or unhealthy.

Whites are at greater risk for anorexia and bulimia than people of color, but the numbers are growing among ethnic groups. Unfortunately, according to a 2005 *New York Times* article, "No reliable numbers exist for how many minority women suffer from eating problems, but experts suspect that cases are increasing" (Brodey, 2005). A soft, round female form is more readily acceptable in the black and Hispanic communities than in the white community, so it makes sense that there is less pressure to be thin and more acceptance of being overweight. Going in the other direction, Asian-American women are no longer as thin as a whole as they once were. Eating and weight problems abound in all racial and ethnic subcultures in this country; however, the greater the exposure of minorities to Western culture, especially in young people, the greater the preference for a thinner body type.

Adolescent females are at the greatest risk for eating and weight problems. The pressure to be thin is strongest in this age group in part because of bodily changes—as girls move into puberty and take on more of a womanly shape—and in part because teenage girls often have few (if any!) normal-sized, healthy public or family role models. Many celebrities of their age and gender are in and out of rehab for eating disorders, and thinness is promoted as essential to popularity and happiness. In addition to the myriad physical changes facing girls between latency and young adulthood, emotional and social changes—higher expectations, more autonomy and responsibility, separation from parents—cause adolescents to feel as if they have little control over their lives. In the face of such helplessness, many young women (and young men as well) focus on what they believe they can control—their weight.

Undoubtedly, saddest of all, is how the quest for thinness and abhorrence of fat has filtered down to young children, predominantly young girls. The National Eating Disorders Association reports that 81% of 10-year-olds are afraid of being fat, that slightly more than half of 9- and 10-year-old girls feel better about themselves if they are on a diet, that the biggest concern of 8- to 13-year-old girls is their weight, and that 80% of all children have been on a diet by the time they reach fourth grade ("Statistics," National Eating Disorders Association Web site). Even for those of us who view slimness and fitness as acceptable goals for adults, these statistics are shocking and frightening because they illustrate the far-reaching effects of our culture's distorted and destructive obsession with thinness.

A population that is often overlooked when considering eating and weight problems is seniors. Anorexia is on the rise for white women as they age, an increase that may be due to the lack of control that comes with the territory—cognitive failures and loss of loved ones and physical capacities—leading to attempts to manage food intake and weight as areas in which we can take charge. Moreover, many single, divorced, or widowed older women competing for a partner in a shrinking pool of them may believe that the thinner they become, the more popular and attractive they will be.

Another group in which concerns are rising about weight and eating disorders is gay males. They have a significantly higher rate of anorexia and bulimia than heterosexual males, and their physical emphasis is as often on being thin as on becoming fit. Suffering some of the same pressures as women, including the need to feel attractive to find a partner, they have responded with increased attention to getting and staying thin and buff.

It is helpful in wondering about which clients might have eating and weight problems to think along the same lines as one does regarding substance abuse. Although we may think of the target population for alcohol and drug problems as young males, we know that we cannot rule out any age group or gender. A 12-year-old girl might smoke pot secretly every morning before middle school and an 86-year-old man might be spending his lonely weekends with a bottle of gin as his only companion. A perky, well-groomed soccer mom may have an addiction to painkillers even as she effectively manages her family, and a high-powered executive may be a cocaine addict nearing bankruptcy and the end of his rope.

In the same way that we look at snapshots or videos of ourselves in youth and may find it hard to imagine or recall being so young, it can be difficult to accept that the popular version of the perfect male and female body was not always as it is now. In a circular fashion, ideals are shaped by historical context and culture even as they impact it. In today's society, ultrathinness is the ideal and messages promoting it are everywhere—hawking cars, hosting TV shows, filling the big and the little screen. Our senses are bombarded with pro-thin, anti-fat messages in the guise of staying fit, attractive, healthy, and youthful, aging gracefully, and living longer. Encased in this time warp, we have to stretch our minds to recognize that thin did not always trump fat and that eating and weight ideals have fluctuated throughout history.

Examining Western art between 1500 and 1900, we see that the idealized woman was not as thin as a walking stick but was round and soft, what today we might genially call pleasantly plump or overweight. Roundness and curves were preferred and considered a sign of opulence and sensuality. Portliness in men—full faces, large waistlines, and big bellies—signified wealth and importance. After all, in the days before the industrial revolution and processed foods, when food was in short supply and a precious commodity, the fatter you were, the richer you were assumed to be. Moreover, a little extra padding ensured survival through regular downturns of food scarcity and famine.

After the industrial revolution and the shift from an agrarian to a more urban-based, manufacturing culture, food became more accessible through rail travel and refrigeration and better tasting through advanced ways to process and preserve it. A growing requirement for food was that it taste good as well as fill up the belly, and quality became as important as quantity. Through marketing and promotion, food began to take on a new aura: no longer merely a physical necessity, it was now consumed for pleasure as well.

At about the same time that technology began to take over the food industry, there was a major shift in standards for American beauty. Dresses had become shorter over time, as first ankles, then knees were bared. The Suffrage movement shoved equality between men and women into the spotlight and gave women a voice they had never had before. To underscore their hard-won freedom, women began to dress differently (perhaps rebelliously), forsaking the traditional ideal of female beauty as curvy and feminine and replacing it with a more masculine look. Toward that end, it was common for women to bind their breasts and wear a short hairdo called a "bob." Gradually, as the decades passed, thinness became de rigueur, as fat went the way of the horse-drawn carriage. Imagine, Lucky Strike commercials used to encourage women to smoke in order to stay slender!

Perhaps as a way of rebelling against women steadily usurping ground in what was previously a male-dominated culture, or in response to the aftermath of the Second World War, when returning soldiers wanted their women to look like, well, *women*, society changed horses once again in the 1950s, and females were once again encouraged to be round and curvaceous. Marilyn Monroe, perhaps *the* female celebrity icon of her time, wore a size 12 dress, and the ideal feminine form was also embodied in movie stars such as Sophia Loren, Jane Russell, Jayne Mansfield, and Mamie Van Doren.

Then, in yet another shift that began today's preoccupation with thinness, in the late 1950s the pendulum began to swing in the opposite direction. A study of Miss America contestants and *Playboy* centerfolds from 1959 to 1988 reported bodies getting thinner and thinner. In the 1960s, a size 2 Twiggy made Marilyn Monroe's size 12 appear positively gargantuan. Since 1979, Miss America contestants have become so skinny that the majority have been well below the recommended weight for their height (Turner, Hamilton, Jacobs, Angood, & Dwyer, 1997). Only recently has the issue of underweight models been addressed in any meaningful way by the fashion industry, and this has occurred only because models were dying from malnutrition, literally self-destructing from being too thin.

Many people struggle with too many or too few pounds at some time during their lives. As we age, metabolism slows and staying trim and/or not putting on weight takes increased effort; female chemistry changes after menopause, making it harder for women to keep off pounds; many new mothers find it hard to slim down after pregnancy; some folks stop eating during periods of upset or upheaval and their weight dips below what is healthy; we may turn to food for comfort and not realize that it is converting itself to fat until our clothes become tight.

It is crucial to recognize that in other times and places, thin was not in. In my "Quit Fighting with Food" workshop, I remind participants that it is unfortunate for most of us that we live in a period in which thinness is so greatly prized. Had we been alive earlier than the 20th century, there is a good chance that the majority of Americans—except for the poor, who were gravely undernourished—would fit right in with the body sizes of those bygone eras. Or, as one morbidly obese workshop participant said, "If I lived on one of those South Sea islands (where fat has traditionally been considered a sign of wealth and prosperity), people would worship me!" Instead, as a 20-something American male, he suffers from what we call poor "body image" due to obesity.

For most of history, body perceptions were not separated out from how people saw themselves in general. There was a greater range of acceptable weights than exist today and most people fell somewhere in the middle. Because of this wider tolerance, people did not attach the same importance to the size and shape of their body as they do nowadays. Sure, some folks might have wished they had more muscles or curves, while others longed for a slimmer waist, larger breasts, broader shoulders, or more height. But for the most part, their sense of self-worth and view of their appearance were not based on weight alone. How they dressed and carried themselves was equally significant, as were occupation, character, intelligence, and personality.

It is one thing for society to have an ideal of what people should be or look like. Having standards and role models is part of human nature and not necessarily a bad thing. However, when the ideal is unreachable by the majority of the population and alone causes severe dysfunction, something is very wrong. Because we live in such a culture, we should expect that many clients who are above the weight norm (and some who are below) will have body image problems. Of course, they may not label them as such. They may joke about their weight or minimize their shame; they may tell us that they are fine with how they look or how much they weigh. They may tell us initially, as one of my clients did, that her extra 100 pounds in no way inhibited her dating, only to share down the road her misery that she felt she had to date whoever was interested in her and be grateful for any interest at all.

A word of caution: It is not true that every overweight client who enters a psychotherapy office has poor body image. Antipathy, however, is something to consider, even when a client initially denies feeling badly about weight or size. Like every other issue, body image needs to be explored, with no response taken at face value. At the other end of the spectrum are clients who will come in and talk about little other than their body hatred. For these obsessed souls, the clinical challenge is to help reduce their negative feelings and increase self-compassion and body acceptance, as well as to gently encourage them to focus on other aspects of self. Too often, body denigration is a bad habit that is unconsciously cultivated to avoid more emotionally explosive or frightening concerns.

One kind of extreme distortion of body image that needs to be addressed in therapy is body dysmorphic disorder (BDD), a preoccupation with real or imagined body defects. This perception often occurs with men and women of normal weight who think they are fat or with those who are ultrathin but still see themselves as chubby. The hallmark of BDD is that it is based on irrational thinking, falsehoods, and lack of evidence. No amount of facts, weight charts, or mirrors will convince someone with such a distorted body image to see themselves clearly and accurately. The problem, obviously, is with perception, not body size.

Treating BDD requires time and patience. It is not enough to tell a client she looks fine and reassure her that she does not need to lose weight, which is generally our first impulse. She is not suffering because she would like to take off 10 pounds, but because her thinking is irrational and dysfunctional and because she will not actually be satisfied when she does lose weight. Instead, she will still consider herself fat and desire to lose even more weight. The disorder is best viewed along the obsessive-compulsive continuum and likely may have biological underpinnings.

A related problem is when a client's self-esteem is based solely on what she weighs. Days are deemed good and bad according to a number on a scale (not even a range of one or two numbers, but a single digit), which translates into how the client feels about herself. She is thrilled when she is at her target weight and in despair when she is even half a pound over. For these clients, weight is everything—never mind the promotion they just received, an upcoming vacation, a marriage proposal, or other events that normally lift spirits. Weight is tied to self-esteem in a pathological way that is hard to understand and sever. Some clients recognize that they have value beyond their body size or shape and benefit from ongoing validation that other aspects of themselves are more important than a number on a scale. Other clients cannot let go of valuing themselves one-dimensionally and will downplay nonweight achievements and trash their significance.

Sadly, for many clients, body image equals self image. Overweight clients may recognize personal and professional accomplishments, but feel a deeply rooted sense of inadequacy, defectiveness, incompetence, and failure because of their size; nothing feels good enough, nothing is important enough to make up for the fact that they are fat. The higher they climb on the professional ladder, the more value appearance takes on; that is, with a higher profile and greater status, they feel even more pressure to look "right" and get their weight under control. It is hard to say whether these clients had low self-esteem to begin with and can tolerate success as long as there is something—their weight—to keep them feeling familiarly badly about themselves, or whether there are factors beyond their control such as heredity and biochemistry (including the link between stress and eating) at work that push their weight above normal.

What I want to stress here is the enormous sense of defectiveness and wrongness that most clients who are overweight feel. I hear frequently that all they want to be is normal, as if a high weight and weight alone makes them abnormal, a kind of subhuman creature who cannot contain her animal excesses. Along with defectiveness comes a sense of defensiveness, a terror of being judged for body size, a dread of being seen as nothing more than a mound of fat (even though that is exactly how they may see themselves), and anxiety about what may be said or implied about them because of their size.

Reflections for Therapist

1. What are your beliefs and assumptions about fatness and thinness? Do you fall prey to any stereotypes?
2. How has culture influenced your attitudes toward weight and body size?
3. Do you need to work on your own attitudes about fatness and thinness to help clients work on theirs?

Although becoming overweight and obese may appear to be the *result* of one kind of eating problem (that is, overeating), and dieting may seem to be the *solution*, this linear, cause-and-effect route is misleading. In fact, dieting is the most common behavior that leads to an eating disorder—some 35% of "normal" dieters will progress to pathological dieting (which is generally a precursor to anorexia and bulimia), and 90% of people who lose weight through dieting will regain more pounds than they originally lost.

Moreover, what constitutes being overweight and obese is not the same today as it was in previous generations. Until recently, people were simply thought of as fat or overweight. Now they are deemed obese if they are more than 20% above the expected weight for their age, height, and body build, and morbidly or malignantly obese if their weight is in excess of 100 pounds above that expected for age, height, and build. Using these public health definitions, approximately 62% of American adults over age 20 are considered overweight, and 32% are judged obese ("General Eating Disorder Fact Sheet," MEDA Web site).

Because weight is not necessarily the best criterion for calculating whether someone is carrying excess weight, body mass index (or BMI), a measure of body fat based on height and weight, is a more accurate evaluative tool. A BMI of less than 19 is considered underweight, while one that is 17.5 or under is labeled as anorexic. A normal BMI is

19–24. At the other end of the spectrum, a person is regarded as over-weight with a BMI of 25–30 and obese with one over 30. Because weight charts and BMI fail to take fitness into account, we must be careful about reading too much into numbers alone: according to BMI and weight, a couch potato is lumped together with a highly active individual such as a construction worker or postal carrier.

It has been drilled into us that being significantly underweight or overweight due to an eating disorder automatically leads to serious, sometimes life-threatening health problems. While this is true for people who suffer from anorexia and mostly true for those who engage in purging, overexercising, diuretics, and laxatives, it is not a hard-and-fast fact. Obviously, people with anorexia cannot be fit and healthy, because they are taking in too few nutrients for their body to function properly, and 1 in 10 cases leads to death ("General Eating Disorder Fact Sheet," MEDA Web site). However, people who are occasionally bulimic may receive enough nutrients to maintain generally good health. They may have other problems, such as tooth enamel erosion due to purging, but may not be malnourished. My point here is not that any of these conditions are part of a healthy lifestyle, but that clinicians cannot take any behavior at face value and must make an assessment in context, taking into account the whole person.

Moreover, recent research tells us that being overweight may not be the killer we have been told it is. A controversial book by *New York Times* science writer Gina Kolata, *Rethinking Thin: The New Science of Weight Loss—and the Myths and Realities of Dieting*, is a must-read for everyone in the health and mental health fields because it details the latest, somewhat surprising, research on obesity (Kolata, 2007). Other recent books have laid out similar arguments and cited similar studies and statistics regarding obesity causing serious and/or life-threatening medical and health problems. See Chapter 4, "Health and Medical Problems," for a description of these problems and the controversy that surrounds how they correlate to weight.

Suffice it to say that there are overweight people who are simply genetically large and who may have a set point or range of weight that is above average. They may not grossly overeat, may choose mostly nutritious foods, and exercise regularly. Keeping this in mind, clinicians should not assume that because a client is heavy, he or she necessarily has eating problems. Although in many cases, clients do—in part because heavy people commonly attempt to diet or restrict calories, which may pack more weight on them in a vicious lose-and-gain cycle—as sensitive practitioners we need to obtain additional information before slapping on an "eating problem" label.

Unfortunately, even when clinicians recognize that clients have food and weight problems, they are often unsure of what to do. As I said in the introduction to this book, both in and out of therapy, the major approach to weight loss has traditionally been dieting. However, because diets do not generally work in the long term—95% of people who diet and lose weight regain it, and 90% regain more than they originally lost—we serve clients best by steering them away from diets when we can ("General Eating Disorder Fact Sheet," MEDA Web site). The only time that a diet is useful and might be successful is when a client traditionally has had a positive relationship with food, has maintained a stable weight for a long period, and wants to lose a small amount of weight, say 5 to 10 pounds, for the right reasons. For example, a client might never have had food or weight problems, but finds that she has put on 6 or 7 pounds after the death of her spouse. Another might gain weight following a move to a new city and a new job. Even in these situations, however, a client is better off thinking about ways to eat less than to put herself on a diet, with its connotations of deprivation and self-denial.

Diets fail to work in the long term because they change only behavior, not thinking. Three therapeutic elements are needed to help clients resolve their problems with food for life. The first is to help clients *shift attitudes* by exploring beliefs about food, eating, appetite, the scale, diets, and their bodies. If beliefs are irrational and unhealthy, the clinician must work with clients to make them rational and healthy before behavioral change will stick. The second is to teach clients who lack a positive relationship with food the *skills to eat "normally"*—eating when they are hungry, choosing foods that are satisfying, eating with awareness and enjoyment, and stopping when they are full and satisfied. The third is to educate clients about emotions to improve *feelings management* that will help them reach their life goals as well as eating and weight goals.

Helping clients overcome food problems and resolve weight issues touches on almost every aspect of their lives—relationships, self-care, childhood socialization, work, play, and family. Even when not exploring food and weight issues, it is a good idea to keep in mind how working through these struggles frees up a client's energy so he or she can focus on other things. Viewing eating problems as integral to, and not separate from, other troubling aspects of a client's life encourages all-around skill development, empowerment, effective self-care, and a positive relationship with the self and others.

Reflections for Therapist

1. What kind of help does the client need regarding beliefs about eating, weight, body, and so on? Is thinking basically rational and healthy or irrational and unhealthy?
2. How close does the client seem to being a "normal" eater, that is, following the four rules regarding starting and stopping eating and making food choices?
3. Does the client appear to be an emotional eater or to withdraw from food to bind anxiety? Is she aware of it? Might the client need work on emotional management before she can tackle her eating problems?

4. How is the client's eating problem representative of other problems in his life?

Our role as practitioners has always been, at least in small part, that of magicians who know what clients are thinking and feeling, so that we can lead them to a higher awareness and more intelligent behavior. Clients often remark on how they feel a skilled therapist can see right through them, not in the sense of making them feel invisible, but in helping them identify what is already there inside them. Obviously, the more a clinician knows about how clients with eating and weight problems feel and think, the more she can work her "magic," which is really a mixture of empathy, insight, and practical wisdom. Learning more about the subject is the first step. Only after we educate ourselves can we educate our clients.

CHAPTER 2

How Clients Express Themselves Through Food

Although we wish to have neutral feelings and objective opinions about size and weight, especially regarding clients, it is virtually impossible as therapists to grow up in this culture and not have a strong predisposition toward thinness and against fatness. What I learned in social work school about color and racism sadly applies to weight as well: Due to institutional cultural bias that permeates almost every aspect of our lives, we all suffer, to a greater or lesser degree, from prejudice against fat people. The best we can do is to acknowledge our preconceptions, try to correct them, and avoid contaminating the therapy hour with them.

In spite of the fact that stereotypes about fatness and thinness are not true across the board, we persist in prejudicial perception because that is the way the mind works—we automatically group folks together in order to anticipate what they will be like. We all have a natural inclination to stereotype, to prejudge others by associating how a person appears with expected behavior. However, because we have that tendency does not mean that it is healthy or productive—especially when it distorts reality.

Another reason we hold stereotypes about fatness and thinness is because we live in a society that unequivocally exalts being thin and despises being fat. Who can pick up a newspaper without reading an article cautioning about the obesity epidemic, thumb through a magazine without noticing promotions for diet programs and weight-loss drugs, or get caught up in TV news segments offering the skinny on bariatric surgery or liposuction? Even at a doctor's visit, the first thing we are asked to do is hop on the scale as our weight is carefully charted in our record.

Moreover, we live in an era in this country and in the "developed" world in which fitness rules. In earlier times, the goals were a roof over our heads, enough to eat, and the well-being of family. Later came the possibility of a little land and perhaps satisfaction and pleasure from work. Life was largely a struggle, and joy and success related to meeting basic needs. Although fitness started out—and even now might be viewed as—a health issue, American culture has made staying in shape and living a healthy lifestyle an end in itself. Our bodies must be pretty and fat free—and preferably youthful. It follows that, in most eyes, folks who by virtue of slimness may *appear* fit trump those who do not. No matter that a heavy person might actually possess more endurance, flexibility, strength, and balance than a thinner counterpart.

Overeaters and undereaters are also pigeon-holed, though often unintentionally. We often assume that overeaters lack self-restraint, live a life of excess, are out of control, and have no idea what is good for them. We presume that undereaters couldn't care less about food or are highly picky and selective, that they are in perfect control, and place a high value on good health. Again, these stereotypes do not hold water. There are overeaters who try to eat nutritiously but eat beyond satiety, and undereaters who eat junk food but little of it. There are undereaters who exert tight control over their eating because, underneath, they feel wildly out of control and are terrified of overeating, and overeaters who are restrained in every area but food. Moreover, there are folks who do not eat much but who chain-smoke (which decreases their sense of taste), and those who have no vices other than food.

It is vital for us to understand the extent to which people are stereotyped for how much they weigh and eat. To start, we must be as objective as possible and not prejudge clients. By recognizing our own biases (painful as that may be), we can attempt to neutralize them and minimize their affect. Because most clients grow up and live in the same culture we do, they often have similar judgments about food and their bodies. On the other hand, if they come from another culture, their views about food, fatness, and thinness might be very different from ours.

Reflections for Therapist

PART 1: To understand how societal messages impact our perception of being thin or fat, think of descriptive words or phrases about fat and thin people. Without judgment, jot down images that come to mind. Most people come up with the following for fat people: *lazy, stupid, earth mother, unhealthy, slovenly, excessive, jolly, mothering, genial, generous, caring,* and *inactive.* Conversely, *cold, selfish, perfect, sexual, hard-driving, fit, rigid,* and *in control* are words commonly applied to thin people. Notice that some terms are positive, others are negative, and a third group could be viewed both ways or as value-neutral.

PART 2: Now consider the people you know who are fat and thin (including yourself). Do any of these descriptions of fat people seem true of thin people, or vice versa? Are there words that could apply to either or both weight groups? Do any of the stereotypes apply to you or other people, that is, are they true? My point is to illustrate that we have unconscious and conscious ideas about weight that are nothing more than prejudices. There are plenty of overweight people who appear jolly but are actually depressed and others who are grumpy inside and out and would probably be that way if they were as thin as a beanstalk. There are control freaks who are large and fat and earth-mother types who are petite and slim. There are folks in both camps who are lazy, generous, stupid, cold, sexual, caring, and hard-driving.

To understand how culture affects a client's perception of being overweight/underweight and being an overeater/undereater, ask:

1. How does the country/culture you grew up in view being overweight/underweight and overeating/undereating?
2. How does your current culture affect your beliefs and behavior?
3. Does this create a conflict?
4. How might you resolve it?

It is useful to recognize how society views weight-challenged people, because some clients play out common stereotypes unconsciously. Of course, not every client acts out against others or herself through food or body size. Sometimes a cigar really is just a cigar, that is, as discussed in Chapter 3, "The Biology of Eating and Weight," many weight and eating problems are primarily due to biological causes and there is little more to them than that. However, it is our job to entertain possibilities and to know the lay of the land, which in this case is both the internal and external pressures that clients yearn to live up to regarding societal body ideals.

In later chapters, we will take a closer clinical look at how to handle behaviors that may get expressed through weight and eating problems. First, though, we must understand how societal perceptions and prejudices often dovetail with client issues. In addition to stereotypes that get projected *onto* people with food or weight problems, there are also *internal* issues with which disordered eaters struggle. Some of these emotional disturbances are conscious, but most are not. They are so interwoven into the fabric of clients' existence and so outside of their awareness that even when we point them out, the client may look at us as if we have two heads and fail to understand what we are talking about.

Feelings about Life Being Unfair

A common conflict that drives disordered eating has to do with underlying anger. Clients may be angry at their metabolism, which they inherited from a long line of overweight overeaters, or at the fact that they are the only family members who are slow calorie burners. Although they may understand cognitively that they did nothing to cause their body to have a particular set point or react to food by putting on pounds, they may become stuck on the unfairness of the situation. Instead of focusing on a window of opportunity to eat more normally and become fit, they resent that they have to work so hard to have a tolerable relationship with food and the scale.

Much of what they feel derives from beliefs about fairness. There is a certain point in the lives of mature adults when they realize that life is truly unfair and, therefore, stop railing against what they cannot change. They accept their dyslexia, diabetes, nearsightedness, arthritis, poor coordination, large nose, or dearth of talent that keeps them from their dream career. This "aha" moment is generally a turning point because they can then stop putting energy into negative thinking, move on, and start creating and enjoying a more satisfying life. However, most of us have had clients who cannot seem to get over this hurdle or who manage to climb over it only to slide backward into resentment and anger when times get tough.

In the eating arena, many clients remain stuck in feelings of injustice because they have a weight or eating problem. They are angry that their sister can eat ice cream every night and not gain an ounce, that their friends can have butter on a baked potato and real cream in coffee, that (what they falsely perceive as) the rest of the world can eat whatever it wants without clothes straining at the seams. Although there is truth in various assumptions (some people most certainly *can* eat more than others because that is how they were genetically engineered), this sense of grievance often precludes recognizing that many, many people struggle with weight and eating and that most of us have to work hard to become and remain fit and be ever vigilant to hold on to a comfortable, healthy weight.

This kind of anger may surface around food allergies. Clients complain about the restrictive choices that being allergic to gluten and dairy imposes on them, their hypersensitivity to sugar and how it seems as if all they need to do is look at a chunk of cheesecake for the scale to creep up a notch. To be sure, it is extremely trying to eat when one has bona fide food allergies—from food shopping to eating out—but the fact is that people who do not have eating problems manage to respond to this inconvenience fairly well. They accept that they are allergic and eat accordingly, albeit with occasional envy, annoyance at limited choices, or yearning for forbidden foods.

The sense of grievance that surges for those who have eating problems *and* food allergies is more about deprivation, helplessness, feeling on the outside looking in, and issues about having choices and getting emotional needs met. This rage gets played out by a client dividing herself in two: One part acknowledges she should avoid a particular food because of health repercussions, while the other part rebels against the unfairness of restriction. Sadly, the client often ends up eating (more likely, overeating) the prohibited food and, consequently, suffering both emotionally and physically.

Feelings about Food and Parenting

Another kind of fury that is often embedded in the unconscious of clients with (over- and under-) eating problems is against parents or primary childhood caretakers (often an aunt or grandmother). Some anger is about food and weight and some is not. For example, clients may become angry because, as children, their food intake was severely restricted. This may have happened because there was insufficient money for groceries or because parents, older siblings, or one special child received more food while other family members received less. The end result is that clients feel deprived and resentful even when they are adults and have plenty of food around.

It is important to remember that poverty is not the only reason that children do not receive adequate food. Sometimes parents are selfish and neglect their children's nutrition while feeding themselves quite well. Often, especially for younger children or girls, older children or "growing boys" get the best of what is on the dinner table, while everyone else is stuck with what remains. Clients who grew up in this kind of household may feel competitive when eating with others, fearing they will not get their fair share. Once again, their conflict is whether to listen to their body and stop eating when full or satisfied, or to overeat and feel as if they are making up for the inequities of the past.

Yet one more type of anger and bitterness arises when parents are hypercontrolling and regularly impose food choices onto children. Clients often feel as if they lacked opportunities to decide if they were hungry, rarely got to choose what they craved, or hardly ever got a chance to eat until they were satisfied. Frequently, these children were fed on a rigid schedule and in such a way that their food needs were barely, if ever, considered. Sometimes they were told that if they did not eat what was put in front of them, they would go without, or that if they did not sit down at the table when dinner was ready that they would go to bed hungry. Additionally, well-intentioned parents may fear that chubby children will grow up to be fat, so they severely restrict portion size, seconds, and treats.

A child who grows up with these kinds of rigid external limitations feels helpless and hopeless that her hunger, pleasure, or fullness needs will ever be met. As an adult, she might take out her anger on herself by consuming foods she really does not want or by stuffing herself just to prove (to herself? her parents? the world?) that she is in control of her nourishment needs. Unfortunately, her conflicting feelings are generally outside her awareness: The conscious, healthy side of her knows she cannot make up for the past, while the unconscious, unhealthy side continues to try to do so.

Not only overeaters, but undereaters (and those who are underweight) may suffer from underlying rage that fuels their eating problems. Children who were forced to eat or finish all their food often rebel in adulthood by eating as little as possible, even though there is no longer a parent standing over them. These rebellions often drive anorexic behavior, as the client's inner "child" continues to wage war with the "adult" by repeatedly saying no to food now in spite of causing physical self-harm.

Feelings about Nonfood Deprivation

Another kind of deprivation and resentment is not about food, but may get displaced onto it. This happens when children are fed adequately and appropriately, but in other ways are neglected or have their needs marginalized, especially emotionally. A parentified child who received little nurturing but had to take care of a brood of siblings while Mom and Dad worked may feel she did not get enough love, guidance, or support, and may angrily act out a sense of greed with food. Conversely, the middle or youngest child may have sorely lacked attention and may try to make up for it by "getting enough" food as an adult, particularly if this food is prepared by someone else (a spouse or a restaurant).

To assess the client's underlying anger regarding food, ask:

1. Do you feel angry when you think about eating?
2. What might make you angry about food or weight?
3. Is there unacknowledged anger, greed, or resentment driving you when you say, "I deserve" a food, and then eat it when you're not hungry?

Feelings about Self-care

Far too many clients suffer from low self-esteem and care for themselves inadequately, especially regarding appearance. It makes sense that clients who were neglected might, in turn, neglect themselves, but this narrow perspective oversimplifies a complex issue. To be sure, there are clients who were mistreated physically or lacked positive attention as children who as adults manifest maltreatment by not caring about how they look. They may be disconnected from their body (through abuse and/or trauma), or may not recognize that proper self-care includes being clean and dressing presentably and appropriately. In fact, they may pay little attention to how they look because they never learned that it mattered.

However, clients who were brushed aside and received little care as children also may overfocus on how they look as adults—clothes, makeup, and hairdo may need to be just so, as if to say, "See, nothing's wrong here." The underlying issue is how poorly these clients feel about themselves when they fail to put extra effort into looking good and when they do not feel they look "perfect." Because they feel unattractive and unlovable enough "as is," they may end up spending enormous amounts of time, money, and energy striving for physical perfection. Their underlying fear is that if they stop being thin or looking attractive, they will lose popularity, status, attention, and, of course, love.

At the other end of the spectrum is the client who was treated poorly in every aspect of life but physical appearance. She may have received scant attention and guidance except in the area of looks, leading her to think that appearance is more important than any other attribute or that it is her only one. Maybe her parents lavished clothes on her and bought her things to make up for not spending quality time with her. Perhaps she had a parent (generally same gender) who believed looks were all *she* had to offer and projected this belief onto her child. Or maybe an opposite-gender parent ignored this child except to fuss over her appearance (perhaps even seductively). Although as clinicians, we may see a well-groomed client sitting before us and think she has excellent self-care skills, she may be covering up a deep and long-standing sense of unworthiness and defectiveness.

By far the most common reaction to poor self-care as it relates to physical appearance surfaces in clients who are trying to make a statement about how little they care about their looks. This declaration may be conscious or unconscious, but its intent is to create an air of "Who cares?" Too often parents impose impossibly high standards of appearance on their children who must at all times be slaves to neatness, good grooming, and cleanliness, and must remain hypervigilant about how they look. Healthy parents want their children to look presentable, but understand that they need to feel free to make a mess and forget about their appearance in the service of letting loose and having fun.

The child who, against her will and inclination, was forced to be

Mom or Dad's little beauty queen or king may take a stand at self-preservation (that is, the autonomous self) by shrugging off how she looks. She may not realize that she is thumbing her nose at a parent's lofty standards or might intentionally dress provocatively (wearing dirty jeans out to dinner, leaving a shirt tucked out at a time when it should be tucked in, wearing ill-fitting clothes or the same clothes day in and day out) in order to upset a parent. Though it may seem as if the client truly does not give a hoot about appearance, her goal is more likely to make a statement about autonomy and send a message about self-rule.

Another common internal conflict gets played out when an adult becomes or remains overweight in order to be unlike a parent. If the parent was constantly on a diet and made the child feel unentitled to eat what and when she wanted, the client may get fat and establish independence through rebellion. This is especially true if a parent withheld food from a child while insisting that it was for her own good (even though it may have been!). This dynamic can also occur when the parent struggles with food herself and tries to make sure her child will be slim by controlling food intake. As resentment builds, often the child packs on the pounds.

Unfortunately, rebellion in the service of separation can often develop into a pattern of poor self-care. Issues of feeding are very delicate, as youngsters are highly sensitive to nuance. It is not necessarily the lack of food or choice that makes the child rebel, but the way in which the parent dominates the child and unilaterally takes away her control. I often ask clients to bring in photos of their families, especially their parents, and am not surprised when an overweight client has a pencil-thin, perfectly coiffed mom or a dad who looks as if he could step off the pages of GQ. In discussing the contrast in appearance between client and parent, what generally surfaces is resentment about being made to look a certain way and lacking the freedom to be or eat differently from Mom or Dad.

One of the most obvious ways that effective self-care gets generated is through a client feeling she is worthy and deserving of looking and feeling good. However, many clients feel woefully undeserving and cannot imagine treating themselves well. They fail to take care of their health or possessions, allow themselves to be taken advantage of, abused, or victimized, are underachievers, and sabotage their best (and others') intentions because of low self-esteem. They operate on the assumption that they should be grateful for the good things that come their way and, even when they try to improve their lot, often undermine or sabotage their endeavors—to eat healthier or establish a comfortable weight—because deep down they do not believe they deserve success.

To understand how self-care issues may relate to the client's eating and weight problems, ask:

1. How do you think you do taking care of yourself?
2. Do you understand how eating too much or little might be a way of not taking care of yourself very well?
3. Is how you look any kind of rebellion against your parents or society?
4. Do you express how you feel about yourself through your weight?

Feelings about Growing Up

Although some clients look as if they are rebelling through their eating or their weight, they really may be expressing ambivalent feelings about becoming autonomous, making their own decisions, and trusting themselves. Clients who are still dependent on their parents well past the age when it is appropriate (because their parents have enabled this behavior) really do have difficulty trusting themselves in the food arena. They are so used to being undermined or, alternately, being overly controlled regarding food decisions, only to be left alone the next moment, that they are truly confused. They have been taught that they cannot count on themselves to meet their needs, food and otherwise.

As such, eating unhealthily by over- or underdoing it is a way to keep parents (or others such as a spouse, partner, friend, or therapist) engaged so that clients can avoid being responsible and accountable for their own feeding. Their conflict is that they both want and do not want the involvement of others. That is, they desperately desire instruction so they can avoid the consequences of making their own mistakes and can blame others when feeding goes wrong (and they gain or lose weight), but also resent a firm hand because it diminishes their sense of independence, competence, and self-trust. They end up acting out their dilemma by gaining or losing weight or having an ongoing eating disorder that keeps others involved in guiding their life.

Feelings about Suffering

Some clients who have suffered trauma either are unable to recover from it sufficiently to let it go or have made it such a central part of their identity that it defines who they are. In cases where a client has survived exceptional neglect, sexual, emotional, or physical abuse (especially at the hands of parents), or numerous significant losses, she may feel that she needs a way to tell people that she has not had an easy life. She may wish more than anything to be "normal" and to have gone through life without trauma, while her history or experience may feel like the only thing that makes her unique and truly special.

One way she may signify to others that she feels different or marked is by continually having problems. If she is grossly overweight or underweight, people may feel sorry for her or fear that she is emotionally vulnerable or fragile and go easy on her. If she has an eating problem, she can keep people involved with her on a controllable level (giving her advice about eating or finding a healthy weight) and still feel connected to the world without engaging in true intimacy. She may see her current food problems as a symbol of all she has suffered and of the bitter life that has made her who she is. Without having to say a word, by her size alone, she may be telling people her most heavily guarded secret or sharing the most sacred part of herself.

Feelings about Sexuality and Intimacy

It is hard to grow up in this culture and feel comfortable in one's own skin and with being sexual. Mixed messages about sexuality abound: Be as attractive as you can be. Don't look too good or it's your fault if you get hit on. You'll only snag a man/woman if you look good. Being fat precludes being/feeling sexual. Being thin means you have to be sexual. You must look muscular and trim to be a turn-on. Revealing your body means you must want to have sex. The way these messages collide and cancel each other out makes a person's head spin. Worse, they make it very confusing to know exactly how to feel about and what to do with the sexual self.

Although there is a high correlation between sexual abuse and eating disorders, most women who have problems with eating or weight were not raped or molested and are not incest survivors. They may not have had specific, negative, traumatic sexual experiences, but by virtue of growing up in this society, they cannot help but internalize the conflicting and confusing messages that are embedded in our culture and institutions: the need for strict school dress codes versus the provocative or scant attire of stars and celebrities; government intervention to restrict contraception and abortion while allowing pornographic images to permeate TV and the Internet; being pushed toward popularity while holding virginity sacrosanct; keeping up sexually with a peer group while practicing safe sex.

Because sexuality generates intense and frightening emotions, it can be easier for a client to use body size as a way to feel safe and secure than to go out in the world as a sexual being or try to contain lustful feelings. In this culture, being extremely under- or overweight desexualizes people to the extent that it often takes them completely out of the social running (in their own or others' eyes). Their unconscious hope may be that if people consider them unattractive, they will be left alone. This does not mean that clients who use weight or size to buffer romantic intimacy do not want to be sexual, only that they have conflicting feelings about it, especially regarding saying no. That is, they may be as frightened of their own sexual desires as those of others toward them.

Similar mixed feelings hold true regarding intimacy, and size can be used as a way to say, "Keep away. Can't you see I'm not available?" The desire to withdraw from relationships may be related to childhood interactions being too intense or too distant or a perplexing yo-yo of the two. A client who had an overbearing, controlling parent may feel engulfed by a push for closeness from another human being; a client with a parent who had no idea how to express closeness or completely avoided being intimate might believe that intimacy in a relationship is unwarranted, unnecessary, or unusual. Using weight to withdraw from interpersonal relationships is generally based on fear of not being able to regulate emotional closeness and distance. Rather than take a chance at having appropriate interpersonal connections and failing, it is easier to opt out completely by having a weight outside the cultural norm.

Being over- and underweight can also be a way the client ensures that she will never get hurt. If she refuses to allow anyone to get close enough to matter, she cannot be rejected or abandoned by them. Maybe she has been through a rough divorce or had a partner who left her for someone younger, or perhaps she has suffered through a series of abusive partners or romantic losses and equates romance with heartache. Either way, weight may be used as an impenetrable shield around her heart.

To assess how the client might be acting out through body size or eating problems, ask:

1. How independent and autonomous do you feel or believe you are?
2. Is it better to be independent or dependent and why?
3. Do you connect past trauma to your eating or weight problems?
4. Does your body size play a part in how you relate to people socially or romantically?

Acting Out and Acting In

Although clients may think of us as mind readers, we know that we are not. We pick up cues and apply principles of psychology to pull the rabbit out of the hat as often as we use intuition to reveal what is inside a client's mind. The only way to verify what is going on with a client, however, is by hearing about and/or observing behavior. Client actions prove our hunches true or false; their patterns of behavior indicate whether a singular act is an anomaly or a manifestation of personality. Whether we start from the premise that a client has distorted thinking or difficulty regulating emotions, or we focus on dysfunctional, destructive behavior, the goal is always to help the client connect her actions with what is going on inside her.

One of the most obvious indications of internal conflict about food and weight is when a client reports that a spouse or partner is helping her stay away from forbidden foods by hiding treats or acting as the gatekeeper to them. I call this behavior, "Save me from myself." In this scenario, to feel more comfortable and secure around food, a client who is unable to say no puts the responsibility on an intimate. What develops is a dependence on the gatekeeper to control the client's food intake and a concurrent resentment that she is unable to do this for herself. A client may also avoid struggling with her food desires by asking a co-worker to hold her treats, again setting up unhealthy dynamics that feel comfortable (and comforting) in the moment but do not serve the client (or the other person) or foster relational health in the long term.

Another dysfunctional way that clients use other people in food struggles is allowing family members or co-workers to sabotage or undermine their efforts to become "normal" eaters and establish a healthy weight. A client will often "blame" someone for tempting her to eat, therefore avoiding taking responsibility for her food choices. She may unconsciously feel relieved that there is someone out there "making" her eat so that she does not have to do battle with her impulses and can give in without acknowledging that she wants to.

Internal conflict about food and weight also gets played out when clients allow family members, friends, or colleagues to make ongoing comments about their weight, even those disguised as pep talks. Comments do not have to be negative to be inappropriate. Each client has a body and that body belongs to her alone. An occasional nudge in the right direction regarding food may be welcome (if invited), but ongoing commentary makes the issue of weight an interpersonal rather than an intrapsychic one. That is, each client has to be her own cheerleader as well as her own gatekeeper. Allowing others to take either role only undermines opportunities to practice saying yes and no to food appropriately, and to feel consequent pride, disappointment, or shame from one's choices.

Another set of unresolved feelings that gets played out in the weight or eating arena relates to being taken care of. When a client puts an intimate in the position of monitoring what is good and bad for her to eat (or weigh), she may actually enjoy the feeling that someone values her enough to take an interest in her health and well-being. She may interpret being scolded for or restrained from eating treats as caring behavior, and to an extent it is. However, true caretaking fosters, but does not take the place of, self-nurturing and self-regulation. Often, a client may not allow people to take care of her in other ways and be dependent on nurturance in the food and weight arena.

A rebellion against weight and eating norms may also surface in relationships when an oversized person feels unlovable at her weight yet expects others to love her as is. In this situation, a client may be saying, "If you *really* loved me, my weight wouldn't matter to you," or "Prove your feelings by loving me at any size." What a client really desires is unconditional love, which is unrealistic for adults to request (although perfectly natural for them to yearn for!). Although people are lovable (or not) in spite of their weight, using weight to test out someone's love is usually done unconsciously. This kind of acting out fails to address the underlying quandary about lovability in the first place or whatever is going on in the relationship that may be causing the client to feel insecure.

Another form of acting out with weight arises when one person in a relationship ends up either actually or symbolically expressing anger or rebellion for the unit. This may happen when one person in a diad is a strict conformist who uses the other person, the client, to act out unconscious feelings of individualism or a desire to buck the norm. The client who has unresolved issues about conforming (most often to what her parents wanted her to be or look like) ends up using her weight to act out this sentiment, and her overweight status, there-fore, becomes a symbol of defiance for them both.

To assess how a client expresses unconscious needs in relation to others, ask:

1. Do you take responsibility for your food and weight issues, or do you sometimes blame others or hold them responsible?
2. Do you have a desire to be loved unconditionally, no matter what your weight is?
3. Are there other unconscious internal conflicts, needs, or fears that you might be acting out through your body size or eating problems?

There is a great deal to consider in deciding whether a client's emotional needs are getting expressed through eating or weight, and the job may feel overwhelming. However, many of these dilemmas are connected to other internal conflicts we already recognize regarding neglect, rebellion, lack of self-love, or autonomy. Unconscious, under-lying conflicts that get played out in the eating or weight arena gener-ally add to what we already understand about a client. Rarely is this new information. When it is—when a therapist first notices a dynamic in the food/weight arena—it is highly likely that it will crop up in other areas of the client's life as well.

CHAPTER 3

The Biology of Eating and Weight

As therapists, we watch as theories about human dysfunction come and go. For a long time, conditions such as alcoholism and drug addiction were viewed and treated according to either a moral or a medical disease model. The understanding and treatment of eating and weight problems have followed along this path as well.

The moral approach maintained that folks who drank in excess or abused drugs lacked willpower and self-control and needed to conquer their impulses (and demons) in order to live a happy, healthy, abstinent life. People were considered to be at the mercy of their addictions until and unless they remained ever vigilant about staying clean and sober. Alcoholics and addicts had to be motivated, keep their eye on the prize, and devote their lives to being in recovery.

The medical model swung public opinion in the opposite direction with its assumption that drug addiction and alcoholism were "diseases" of the body, not the mind. Drunks were thrown into jail to dry out, as if purging alcohol from their cells would ensure their body's proper functioning from then on. Addicts were shut away to kick their habits in the hopes that pains of withdrawal would be enough to keep them clean. In these scenarios, we can almost picture a demon rising up from a body and vanishing into thin air, leaving behind a purified and healthy soul.

A subsequent school of thought maintained that addictions were caused by family dysfunction, just as schizophrenia and autism were thought to be the result of inadequate parenting. Disenable the enablers, help children separate appropriately from their families, get them talking in therapy, and their substance abuse problems would be resolved. There was also a time when we believed that recovery would grow out of being educated about substance abuse: See how you're hurting yourself, tell yourself you're worthy of sobriety and you won't have that drink, share your shame and remorse, buddy up, and your desire for drink or drugs will gradually leave you.

Although food fails to fit neatly into the category of addiction and disordered eating is not a disease per se, there are many similarities in the way food and substance abuse problems have been viewed and treated over the decades. Fortunately, science is acquiring knowledge by leaps and bounds about the underlying roots of many diseases and conditions, and we now understand that there are biological causes for many addictions, along with social and cultural counterparts.

Nowhere is this truer than in the field of eating and weight. We have already touched on some dysfunctional family dynamics that occur in childhood that may generate and promote eating problems (low self-esteem leading to poor self-image and self-care, excessive restriction producing feelings of deprivation, ineffective emotional management spawning emotional eating, the regular use of treats as reward teaching misuse of food, and nonnutritional family eating con-tributing to ignorance about a healthy diet). Although parental atti-tudes—and those of other relatives who are involved in child-rearing—toward food and weight are a large contributor to a client's ability to eat "normally" and maintain a comfortable weight, socialization is only part of the story.

The rest is what we come into the world with—that is, our genetic makeup. In fact, a recent controversial theory maintains that 70% of our weight may be genetically determined (Kolata, 2007). You may be surprised—and dismayed—to learn that so much of a client's (or your own) weight is fixed. Although many clients respond with disappointment, frustration, anger, and hopelessness to the realization that there is a limited amount they can do to reduce their weight, other clients feel validated and relieved. This statistic relieves the huge burden of believing they have not tried hard enough and do not have the gumption to stay slim. These folks have struggled unsuccessfully their whole lives to achieve or maintain a target weight (or weight range), and have never understood what they were doing wrong when the pounds crept back on. Instead of blaming their biology, they faulted their lack of willpower or motivation.

Only in the second half of the last century did science come to realize that the subject of eating and weight is about as complex as they come (right up there with addictions). The topic is complicated by the fact that, although we can stop drinking and taking drugs and enjoy life, we cannot stop eating or we will die. The most important point to remember when talking with clients about eating or weight is that *because all of us start off at a different place in terms of biology, we cannot all end up at the finish line together*. This truth is what diet proponents—and doctors, too often—do not say. Perhaps they fear that clients will never try to shed pounds if they realize that there are limits to how low their weight can go. Or perhaps, like therapists, they simply wish that they and their clients had more power to reach life-enhancing goals.

There are a number of ways that biology impacts the eating styles and habits of clients and their ability to achieve a particular weight. Although each theory about weight that comes along does not apply to every client, it is incumbent upon us as treaters to become relatively conversant with what science has to say about appetite and weight management.

Reflections for Therapist

1. What do you believe causes overeating and being overweight?
2. How does the idea that 50–70% of weight is genetically determined affect your thinking about helping clients change unhealthy eating patterns?
3. How could you present information about the biology of appetite and weight to clients so that they can understand and use it (handouts, book suggestions, etc.)?

Metabolism

Metabolism is the process by which living things turn food into energy. This energy is commonly measured in calories (the quantity of heat needed to raise by 1°C the temperature of 1 gram of water). This energy is then used to build new cells and tissues, provide heat, and produce fuel for physical activity.

To understand the concept of metabolism, think of the relationship of calories in and energy out. Of course, human metabolism is far more complex than such a simple equation, which is why some people do not consume a great many calories and still grow fat, and others appear to eat nonstop and stay trim. This difference is due to variations in individual physiology that influence how much energy a person consumes, expends, and stores as fat.

Animal and human studies over the past several decades have made great strides in understanding weight regulation, but it seems that every answer raises new questions. There is not even a consensus on the workings of regulating weight. Some research points to a popular explanation called set point theory (SPT), which holds that our bodies are preprogrammed genetically to maintain a certain weight and that we cannot remain for long either above or below this limit. SPT calls to mind a thermostat that keeps temperature steady within a range—switching off when the air reaches specific maximum and minimum points. SPT states that when the body's "fat-o-stat" reaches its lowest setting due to voluntary or enforced food reduction, it automatically slows down its metabolic rate to conserve calories. These conserved calories are then stored as fat.

In terms of evolution, this process is highly efficient and human friendly; it is how our species has survived during famine and times of extreme caloric restriction. Some researchers maintain that the human body's regulatory mechanisms may even be inclined toward conserving calories and preserving fat rather than eliminating it. Remember, our bodies have been hardwired through millennia for survival and our species has flourished because metabolism has been adaptive to changing food environments. In lean times, survival of the fittest meant survival of the fattest.

SPT is one way of explaining why many heavy people fail to reach or maintain a target weight: Due to dieting, their body's metabolism slows down, storing more fat and making it virtually impossible, no matter how little they eat, for their weight to dip lower. Additionally, researchers have found that once restriction ends, at least in animal studies, the organism experiences increased hunger and eats more until its prerestriction weight is reattained. These studies underscore an important point to remember in treating overweight clients— *willpower cannot override biology*. SPT also accounts for how people who seem to be able to eat large amounts of food (or high-calorie foods) do not gain weight. When caloric intake exceeds their high-end set point, their bodies actually increase metabolism to burn off the extra calories so that they are not converted into stored fat (pounds). Unfair, but that is how some bodies work.

Research suggests that individual set points are influenced by many factors, including genetics, age (set points tend to increase with age), lifestyle (sedentary versus active), diet, smoking, and exercise (regular aerobics can lower set points). Challengers to this theory maintain that set point is not as fixed as previously assumed; during dieting and weight loss, metabolism may slow down, but once food consumption returns to normal, metabolism, too, returns to prerestriction levels. Challenges also suggest that physical activity plays a larger than heretofore thought role in modifying set points, which means that people can actually reduce their set point by increasing exercise.

Body Structure/Type

Not just metabolism, but body and bone structure influence size and shape. A person who is 6′2″ and weighs 220 pounds will look very different from another person of the same weight who is only 5′4″. Moreover, some folks are broad-shouldered and thick-boned (think football players), while others are small-boned and compact (think jockeys), while yet others are lithe and leggy (think dancers). Height and body structure are strongly influenced by ethnicity as well: the Japanese body type is, on the whole, different from that of the Mexican or Scandinavian. One look at a multigenerational family photo will show most people what they are likely to look like in years to come.

We all work within our limits—short, medium, or tall, small- or large- or long-boned; long-waisted or legged; petite, stocky, or athletic—and it is vital to remember that, for the most part (and except through surgery), we cannot do much to change our body build.

Appetite Regulation

Although the regulation of appetite is strongly influenced by metabolism, the equation of calories in and energy out is only one facet of the story. Most of what we know about appetite regulation comes from animal (generally rat) studies, but appears to pertain to humans as well. Moreover, because researchers often work with very different aspects of the appetite puzzle, at this point it is difficult to understand how all the parts fit together. In fact, it may be decades before scientific understanding is complete and comprehensive enough to use the information gleaned from animal studies to apply to human appetite in any meaningful way.

Appetite and weight are regulated by the brain through chemicals that bring it information about the body's energy and fuel needs. The brain acts like a store's computer by processing data on whatever inventory is available and what stock is needed by customers at any given moment. Just as a store owner may increase or decrease inventory according to customer demand, the brain regulates stores of fat in relation to the body's energy needs. When more energy is needed, more food needs to be taken in, and the brain stimulates appetite. When no more energy is needed and enough fat is available, the brain sends out messages of satiation. The brain may also lower or raise the body's overall energy needs according to what is in its fat stores (that is, it burns more when there is plenty of fat and less when stores are reduced). It can even reallocate energy away from nonessential body systems so that energy is conserved for survival.

The hypothalamus is the region of the brain best known for energy-related activities such as sensing hunger and satiation. What we call appetite regulation happens during the hypothalamus's ongoing assessment of chemical comings and goings. At its simplest, the main components of this chemical information system are ghrelin, which is produced in the stomach and signals that the stomach is ready for a meal, and hormones such as leptin and insulin, which act on cell receptors to influence hunger. Leptin and insulin also have another role on this information grid: Along with glucose and peptides

PYY (peptide tyrosine tyrosine) and cholecystokinin (CCK), they promote satiety while suppressing appetite.

The above description of hunger and satiation is rudimentary. In reality, there are many more chemicals involved in triggering and stopping eating, and the way they work is both subtle and complex. When all these chemicals exist in the correct balance and proportion and do their job well, we receive just the right amount of food to maintain a healthy weight for our lifestyle. However, when these chemicals are lacking or out of balance and fail to do their job, appetite becomes disregulated and we have difficulty managing weight.

Our bodies establish levels of these chemicals in part by what is passed along to us in our genetic makeup. If we are fortunate, we get a balanced complement of appetite regulators; if not, an imbalance may generate weight problems. Regulation of chemicals like ghrelin and leptin, however, is not the only way that genes play a part in determining weight. Through scans of genomes (the complete data about heredity that is encoded in an organism's DNA), scientists have found certain gene mutations that are linked to obesity. The discovery of these genes illustrates that genetics can predetermine our tendency toward obesity or slimness and sets us up for weight management success or failure. It is unclear exactly how these genes interact with the environment to generate a specific weight or range, but it is generally accepted that genes strongly influence body weight through mechanisms not yet fully understood.

Neurotransmitters

Most of us are familiar with the terms *neurotransmitters* and *neuromodulators*, especially if we treat clients who take medication for anxiety or depression. These are chemicals that relay, amplify, and modulate electrical signals between a neuron and another cell, biochemical agents that transmit information from one cell to another to regulate mood and affect. Clinicians may be most familiar with the neuromodulator serotonin, which exerts a soothing influence on unpleasant emotions. Other frequently mentioned chemicals are the neuromodulators dopamine, which regulates bursts of intense concentration and feelings of euphoria; norepinephrine, which causes generalized, sustained alertness; and the neurotransmitter gamma-aminobutyric acid (GABA), which promotes relaxation.

In order to understand the connection between appetite regulation and neurotransmitters, we have to step back and examine how the brain works in terms of pleasure and reward. Sigmund Freud may have erred in many of his theories, but he was spot on when he posited that human beings move toward pleasure and away from pain. Now science is able to identity the specific brain circuitry that registers pleasure and is stimulated by, among other activities, eating.

Food is meant to taste good and bring us pleasure or we would not eat it or enough of it to stay alive. It makes sense that the brain would register delight in food and that this pleasant feeling would be recalled and associated with what we have ingested. Further, it makes sense that foods that would contribute most to our survival would be high in fat, sugar, and calories (leading to fat storage) so that we would be attracted to them and eat more of them.

One way that pleasure registers in the brain is through the release of dopamine. When we eat a chocolate-glazed doughnut, the subsequent pleasurable burst of dopamine we feel makes it likely that we will reach for this same food again and again. Because of their chemical makeup, carbohydrates raise serotonin levels naturally and act as natural tranquilizers. In fact, some experts think that individuals who crave carbohydrates have a low level of serotonin and turn to carb-rich foods to help regulate their moods.

— —

Food Addictions

It is interesting to ponder whether food could be said to have addictive properties—through natural or chemically added ingredients—or if compulsive eaters merely feel as if they are addicted. Although there are adherents on both side of this debate, the scientific jury is still out. Traditionally three criteria have been used to establish addiction: (a) increased tolerance of a substance demands that more of it be ingested to achieve a "high"; (b) psychological cravings for a substance must be in evidence; and (c) physiological withdrawal symptoms must be felt in the absence of a substance.

Research has shown that eating certain foods can increase dopamine levels in the brain, but this elevation is not enough to prove that food is addictive. It only suggests that specific foods register in the reward circuitry of the brain in much the same way as alcohol and some drugs. There also is evidence that rats appear to become addicted to sugar water, but it is not clear that the problem is not one of psychological dependence rather than addiction, there being such a thin line between the two.

The problem with using the addiction model with food is knowing how to respond even if physical dependence exists. Identifying a substance as addictive is helpful when users have a choice regarding its usage, as with drugs and alcohol. But to tell clients to completely abstain from eating carbohydrates, the foods that are often viewed as addictive, is another story. First of all, we need to eat some carbohydrates to remain healthy, and second, shunning fat and sugar, the "addictive" components of carbohydrates, most often leads to deprivation and rebound eating.

— —

Food Allergies

Related to the topic of food addiction is food allergies. Typical food allergies include wheat (gluten), soy, dairy (milk), eggs, peanuts, and shellfish.

According to the Food Allergy and Anaphylaxis Network, about 4% of Americans—more than 12 million—have food allergies characterized by an adverse reaction triggered by the immune system ("Food Allergy Facts and Statistics," available from the Food Allergy and Anaphylaxis Network Web site). In a bona fide food allergy, the immune system mistakenly identifies a specific food or a component of a food as a harmful substance, causing cells to make antibodies to fight the culprit food or food component (the allergen). When an individual eats even the smallest amount of that food, the antibodies sense it and signal the immune system to release histamine and other chemicals into the bloodstream.

Symptoms of a food allergy usually develop within an hour after eating the offending food and may include hives, itching, eczema; swelling of the lips, face, tongue, and throat, or other body parts; wheezing, nasal congestion, or trouble breathing; abdominal pain, diarrhea, or nausea; and vomiting, dizziness, light-headedness, or fainting. Other reactions do not involve the immune system (and consequent release of histamine) and are not allergies but food intolerances. Because they may cause many of the same symptoms as allergies—nausea, vomiting, cramping, and diarrhea—people often confuse the two. Food intolerances may make an individual uncomfortable, but they are not valid allergic reactions. Common allergens are milk, eggs, peanuts, tree nut, seafood, shellfish, soy, and wheat.

Clients often insist that they have a food allergy because they "cannot" stop eating a certain food. Offending foods are often carbohydrates that are high in sugar and/or fat. Current research suggests that people who eat sugar and crave more of it do *not* have an allergy to sugar, in spite of the fact that eating it may trigger a craving for more. The only way clients will know if they have a food allergy is to be tested by a health professional.

Asking clients about their reaction to certain foods will help them start making a connection between ingestion and their physical response. It is important that clinicians stay neutral about the veracity of food allergies and addictions and that we encourage clients to seek medical testing and advice to get answers. Some clients will insist that they have food allergies, while others may have never considered the possibility. Our role is to aid clients in getting to the truth. More information about how to assess and address food allergies and addictions can be found in upcoming chapters.

To help the client identify food allergies, ask:

1. Are there foods you think you might be allergic to?
2. What physical reactions do you have when you eat these foods?
3. Have you talked with your doctor about these reactions?
4. Would you consider getting tested to find out if these are true allergies?
5. If you don't have an allergy to foods you overeat, why else might you have trouble with them?

Weight Loss Through Diet Programs and Plans

Initial theories about weight loss were based on the simple premise of eating less. They were made slightly more complex by adding the instruction to exercise more, based on trying to balance the equation of calories in and energy out. However, we now know that there is much more to weight management than simply counting calories. Science has proven that *what* we eat is as important as *how much* we eat.

Although various weight-loss plans and programs abound, the basic message of healthy eating remains virtually the same as it always has been: Eat smaller portions composed mainly of fruits, vegetables, and whole grains (except if you are allergic), choose unprocessed rather than processed foods, and take it easy with edibles that are high in salt, fat, sugar, and artificial additives.

To explore and critique even the most popular diets of the last decade is beyond the scope of this book, but it is vital that clinicians have an understanding of what clients with eating and/or weight problems go through in order to avoid getting fat, to lose weight, or to keep it off. For some clients, dieting takes over their life, consuming most of their attention and energy. It dictates their social life and has the characteristics of other addictions. For others, dieting is an on-again-off-again romance: Weight is lost and regained, body fat is subtracted and added. Some dieters stick to one plan alone and return to it over and over. Others go from plan to plan in the hopes of finding the magic cure. Dieters may be on a formal plan, become members of a program and attend weekly meetings, or merely count calories or fat grams in the comfort of their kitchen.

In terms of approaches, low-fat diets have long been popular and brought on the advent of hundreds of low- or no-fat products that fill our supermarket shelves. Unfortunately, while the idea seemed to make sense, it turns out that people have a very difficult time sticking to reduced-fat diets. Moreover, fat restriction and physical and emotional deprivation often cause rebound overeating or binge eating high-fat foods.

Some weight-loss plans are based on sound medical and nutritional research, while others have little or no scientific underpinnings.

Moreover, diets that were based on what was solid evidence at one time often fall out of favor when science produces new or challenging information. Although quite a number of diet gurus have done extensive research to make their cases and appear to sincerely want to help people stay fit and healthy, it is sadly obvious that other diet proponents' claims are ludicrous and that these pseudo-experts are only taking advantage of gullible people desperate to be thinner.

There is no end to weight-loss approaches. There are diets that say to eat little or nothing from entire food categories and others that promote eating from only one or two groups. There are plans based on personality, activity level, lifestyle, blood type, or biochemistry as well as ones that must be followed in rigid phases. Some programs require purchasing prepackaged foods or adding specific supplements to a food program. Nowadays, most well-publicized diets include purchasing a book and following what it says religiously.

There is nothing to say that a diet must even include real food. Shakes, which purportedly provide the dieter with a complete nutritional package, may take the place of meals or act as a replacement for a meal or two. Fasting, which involves taking in nutrients through prepackaged drinks or supplements, may function as a way to jumpstart a diet or be used as an approach of last resort.

Because overeating has been viewed similarly to overdoing it with alcohol or drugs, it is not surprising that the most popular treatment model is based on substance abuse recovery, that of individual counseling and/or group support. Weight Watchers, Jenny Craig, LA Weight Loss, and Overeaters Anonymous all have combinations of weigh-ins, counseling, and member-to-member support. These programs include any or all of the following: controlled food intake through behavioral dos and don'ts, abstinence from certain foods, counting calories or fat grams, weighing food, keeping a food journal, reducing portion size, raising awareness about eating behaviors, changing one's attitude toward food, and daily encounters with the scale.

Nowadays, theories about weight loss are being churned out and overturned at breakneck speed, and it seems that the more scientists learn about eating and weight, the better they understand that *there is no one-size-fits-all approach to taking and keeping weight off*. Appetite and body size are highly idiosyncratic, and programs that successfully promote maintaining a healthy, comfortable weight must not only be realistic and doable, but need to take into account an individual's culture, biology, genetics, gender, age, and lifestyle.

To explore the client's diet history, ask:

1. Could you describe the diets you've been on, including how you felt being on them, how much weight you lost, and how long you were able to keep it off?
2. What was the hardest thing about staying on a diet?
3. What was the thing you liked most about dieting?
4. Do you understand how dieting can cause rebound eating and make you fat?
5. Even if you don't diet, are there any aspects of dieting that you could use in achieving and maintaining a healthy weight?

Hormones and Eating/Weight

There are a number of hormonal conditions and diseases of which clinicians need to be aware because they may cause weight gain. If you suspect that a client has a hormonal imbalance, you can review and discuss symptoms together and suggest she talk with her doctor. Some clients may be relieved that there is a medical problem causing weight gain or preventing weight loss, but remember that many clients will be frightened at the thought that there is some "wrong" with them, so tread lightly.

There is the possibility (suggested by research, but unproven) that weight and body fat increase during the decade following menopause. You and your client might think in this direction if she tells you that she has been slim her entire life and only put on weight since she stopped menstruating. In this case, she will benefit from having her hormones tested to see if an imbalance may be causing increased weight.

Hypothyroidism, a condition in which the thyroid gland produces too little hormone, slows down metabolism and may cause weight gain. Symptoms may include coarse and thinning hair, dry skin, brittle nails, a yellowish tint to the skin, slow body movements, cold skin, inability to tolerate cold, feeling tired or weak, memory or concentration problems, constipation, heavy or irregular menstrual periods that may last longer than 5 to 7 days, goiter (enlarged thyroid gland), swelling of the arms, hands, legs, feet, face (particularly around the eyes), hoarseness, and muscle aches and cramps ("Hypothyroidism: Topic Overview," available from the WebMD Web site).

Cushing's syndrome, when the adrenal glands produce too much cortisol, leads to fat buildup in specific areas of the body. Symptoms may include a round or puffy ("moon") face, increased fat around the neck and upper back, or enlarged waistline; thin, fragile skin that bruises easily, slow-healing wounds, ruddy complexion, purplish stretch marks across the body; irritability, anxiety, insomnia, and sadness; backache, broken bones, loss of muscle tone or strength; menstrual irregularity, facial hair growth in women, erection problems in men, loss of sex drive; and hypertension ("Cushing's Syndrome: Symtoms," WebMD Web site).

Polycystic ovary syndrome (PCOS) is the result of a hormonal imbalance that produces an increase in fat cells. Symptoms include fertility and menstrual problems, acne, weight gain or trouble losing weight, extra facial and body hair or thinning scalp hair. Metabolic syndrome (also known as syndrome X) is a cluster of health conditions related to insulin resistance and metabolism disregulation. Symptoms include obesity, high blood pressure, high cholesterol levels, and resistance to insulin. PCOS, getting older, lack of exercise, and abdominal obesity are also associated with Syndrome X ("Polysystic Ovary Syndrome–symptoms," WebMD Web site).

Medications and Eating/Weight

Unfortunately, various prescriptions drugs—including oral contraceptives, steroids or hormone replacement therapy, and diabetes, antidepressants, antiseizure, migraine and blood pressure drugs—may cause weight gain in certain individuals, although studies do not confirm that this is true across the board. Because the use of these drugs is on the upswing and it is likely that many clients are on one or more of them, it is crucial for clinicians to help them assess whether medications are affecting eating or weight. Clinicians also need to be on the lookout for medications that cause weight loss. Because some prescription drugs react idiosyncratically, they may generate weight gain in one individual while causing weight loss in another.

Generally the potential for weight gain (or loss) is written on the printed material that accompanies prescription medications. However, not every reported side effect will be listed. Weight-related information may be available in a *Physician's Desk Reference* (PDR) or from a client's doctor, pharmacist, or the company that manufactured the medication. In cases where clients' self-report is reliable, it is possible that weight gain is a by-product of a medication they are taking, although it is not listed as such. Clients should always be encouraged to discuss problems with medication, and certainly the discontinuation of them, with their prescribers.

Other Influences on Eating and Weight

As if heredity and biochemistry are not enough to consider, there are other factors that may contribute to how people eat and how much they weigh. If a client is under substantial stress at home or on the job, she may be reaching for food in an attempt to alleviate stress. Lack of sleep also may increase the production of appetite-stimulating hormones while decreasing the output of hormones that signal satiation.

To assess causes and contributors to eating and weight problems, ask:

1. When was your last medical checkup that included hormone testing?
2. Have you talked with your doctor about the possibility that you might have an underlying hormonal problem that is affecting your eating or weight?
3. How much sleep do you get at night? Do you know that not getting enough sleep might affect your ability to lose weight? How is your sleeping?
4. Do you understand that a substantial amount of stress may be causing you to reach for food? Do you have a stressful life?
5. Have you thought about other ways to deal with stress or ways to reduce your stress level?

There are theories asserting that the escalating weight of Americans is due to everything from pollution to air-conditioning and heating. Toxic air and chemicals may alter our hormones, while indoor climate control keeps our body at a steady temperature so that it need not "work" to heat up or cool down. Ironically, even the fact that fewer Americans smoke than ever before may be a factor in increasing obesity rates because reduced nicotine intake has been correlated to increased eating. It may even be true that obese people are more fertile than lean ones, which would lead to there being more obese people in every generation.

In decades to come, as scientific research focuses more closely on appetite and weight, we will likely learn that both are influenced by a combination of factors that include heredity, environment, socialization, and biochemistry. For now, it is vital that clinicians help clients understand that there is a strong biological component governing appetite and predicting weight. It is our job to help clients assess whether they have underlying illnesses and conditions that contribute to eating and weight problems, and move them toward getting testing and treatment. Clients should not make the mistake of holding themselves 100% accountable for their weight struggles, but must put their energy into doing whatever is possible to become healthy and fit.

CHAPTER 4

Health
and Medical
Problems

I t is practically impossible these days to pick up a newspaper
or magazine, turn on the television, or check Internet head-
lines without being hit with information on how to feed and take
care of our bodies. We are barraged with results of studies advising
us what foods to eat and avoid, flooded with cautions about the dangers of being overweight or obese, hounded to eat more nutritiously,
and bombarded with suggestions on how to food shop, cook, and
exercise for optimum health and longevity. Trying to keep abreast of
the latest news on decreasing free radicals and increasing fiber, the
benefits of organic foods, the hazards of pesticides, and the health
claims of dark chocolate, green tea, and red wine sometimes seems
like a full-time job.

Moreover, due to the nature of scientific study and the lag time
between conclusions and publication and dissemination of results, it
is not unusual for research that is true today to be proven false tomorrow. Nor is it uncommon for research projects to contradict and even
disprove one another. Many studies are longitudinal and take decades
to produce results, and often, conclusions must be replicated before
they are considered valid. The most reliable and accurate studies are

those that use a double-blind approach and are funded by independent, unbiased laboratories—not the citrus growers studying oranges or a pharmaceutical company researching weight-loss drugs. In fact, the most useful information generally comes from meta-analyses of numerous studies over time.

If mental health practitioners cannot keep up with all that is going on in allied health professions (including biochemistry, fitness, and nutrition), how can clients, many of whom are burdened with depression, anxiety, personality and psychotic disorders, and extraordinary stresses? Although we can try to be well informed, many of our clients are barely squeaking by financially, socially, or emotionally and have no time for or interest in following the latest news on health care. Often they rely on us, along with their doctors and other professionals, to tell them how to take care of their health. That makes it important for us to recognize in broad terms what promotes good health and what harms it, what clients can do to develop a healthier lifestyle and what is out of their control.

Because we must view an individual holistically, therapists can no longer treat only the mind and ignore the body. While we cannot be expected to know the ins and outs of nutrition (I don't and I am in a closely associated field), it is reasonable to expect us to become acquainted with the basics of nutrition, the benefits of exercise, and the health risks of being over- and underweight. This is especially true now that we know beyond a shadow of a doubt that the foods we eat and the lifestyle choices we make have a huge impact on our moods, thinking, and behavior.

Educating clients about the risks of being over- and underweight and malnourished assists them in several ways. First, helping clients understand that they are at risk due to weight-related health problems may gently nudge them out of denying that dysfunctional eating has no negative consequences. It is our job to keep stoking the fires of discomfort so that they do not slip back into denial and forget that they are responsible for their actions. Second, talking about nutrition and malnutrition gives clients opportunities to make small decisions even when they are unwilling to completely overhaul their eating habits. They may seek a nutritional consult, begin taking vitamins, or have their cholesterol tested. Even small changes like these may start the ball rolling in the right direction.

Health Problems Related to Being Underweight or Undernourished

Because a client is thin or underweight (or has a minimum BMI) does not indicate that he is either healthy or unhealthy. A slim client may have a tiny appetite, may eat only small amounts of nutritious foods, have a job that keeps him active, and/or exercise regularly. Or he may just be metabolically lucky! Neither he nor we can decide if he is of sound body unless he has regular checkups, including age-related screenings and blood work. A slender client who fails to exercise may or may not be healthier than one who exercises but remains overweight.

It can be difficult to assess current or future medical problems of clients who are underweight because so much of the health information we receive warns of obesity risks, with very little information (other than what we know about the dangers of anorexia and bulimia) pertaining to low weights. Moreover, a client who is underweight may not be anorexic and may wholeheartedly believe that keeping a low weight is what he is supposed to do to stay healthy. Because so many Americans carry around excess pounds, it makes sense that most medical warnings are geared to this population. Unfortunately, for those who intentionally seek ultraslimness, this message comes across in black and white as fat is unhealthy and thin is healthy, and clients who are underweight may not think of themselves as candidates for malnutrition or medical maladies.

Health problems of underweight clients vary according to the reason their weight is low. There is a world of difference between how we would treat a client who intentionally rigidly restricts her food intake in order to be pencil thin and another who remains underweight because she regularly runs late and skips breakfast, lives on coffee and cigarettes, or forgets to eat because she is too scattered and overwhelmed. We might consider the first client to have an eating problem, and the second to lack adequate self-care skills. However, both might have a BMI of 18.5 or lower, which is considered underweight and may endanger health.

While neither client might meet a diagnosis of anorexia nervosa—the refusal to maintain a minimum, healthy weight—both are putting their physical welfare in jeopardy by weighing too little. Health problems may include anemia, nutrient deficiencies, heart irregularities, delayed wound healing, loss of skin elasticity, diminished immune response, amenorrhea (loss of periods for women), bone loss and osteoporosis, decreased muscle strength, trouble regulating body temperature, difficulty fighting off infection and disease, and even increased risk of death ("Anorexia Nervosa," Mayo Clinic Web site). Moreover, any client below minimum weight who fails to meet weight criteria for anorexia might still have serious psychopathology that compromises her health.

It is possible that the restrictive eater might eat more nutritiously than the "forgetful, scattered" one, so that even if she has a below-minimum BMI, she likely will be in better general physical shape because of higher-quality food choices. We need to take care not to focus only on a client's weight as an indicator of ill health, but must look at what and how much she eats (and, of course, whether the food stays down) as well as the lifestyle choices she makes. It is crucial that we and the client know the cause of her being underweight, especially because conditions such as cancer, HIV, Crohn's disease (a lifelong inflammatory bowel condition), and celiac disease (a condition in which the body's immune system responds to gluten by damaging the lining of the small intestine) may cause initial weight loss (without other major symptoms) and lead to further medical problems.

To assess if the client might have a medical/health problem causing low weight, ask:

1. Do you find that you eat a normal amount, even a lot, but are unable to maintain a healthy weight? How long has this been going on?
2. Have you considered that you may have an underlying medical condition that is keeping your weight low?
3. Does Crohn's disease or celiac disease run in your family?

Health Problems Related to Being Overweight

Scientific literature typically describes a "J-shaped curve," emphasizing that most mortality is associated with obesity rather than being underweight. However, there are recent challenges to these conclusions, such as: "Thus overweight status (BMI ≥ 25.0) was associated with longevity due to lower mortality from cardiovascular disease in very elderly subjects, whereas underweight was associated with short life due to higher mortality from cancer." ("Overweight Associated with Longevity in an 80-year-old Community-based Population," Metabolic Syndrome Institute Web site) and "In conclusion, overweight status in an 80-year-old population was found to be associated with longevity and underweight status with short life" ("Association Between Body Mass Index and Mortality in an 80-year-old Population," Medscape Web site). It is surprising for most of us to learn that, in some cases, being overweight correlates with longevity and under-weight with higher rates of mortality.

A more accurate assessment of weight risk may be found in a March 5, 2008, *New York Times* article: "The curve for risk, in terms of weight, is a bell-shaped curve. . . . There is an ideal weight, above and below which your risks increase. We know about the risks when you're above. The problem is, we don't know what the increased risk factors are with the other side. But the all-out result is that our longevity is reduced" (Blumenthal, 2007, 1). This quote tells us that we should be concerned about the risks of obesity, but that the subject is more com-plicated than we would like to think and that we should be very care-ful, as clinicians, not to pass on misinformation to clients.

Rather than lecture or use scare tactics with heavy clients, we are better off explaining that conclusions are confusing and contradictory and stating right off the bat how much we know about the subject. If we have limited knowledge, we need to say so. We also must make clients aware that doctors are not omniscient gods and that the subject of weight and appetite is enormously complicated and cannot be reduced to simplistic sound bites. Last, we must encourage clients to take responsibility for themselves by staying abreast of new information about weight, eating, nutrition, health, and longevity as best they can.

That said, the major medical consensus today is that being over-weight or obese can lead to any number of serious conditions and dis-eases that may severely reduce the quality of life and decrease longevity. There is no end to the number of books, Web sites, study results, and articles warning about the dangers of unhealthy eating and carrying around excess pounds. For instance, according the the U.S. Department of Health and Human Services, "an estimated 300,000 deaths per year may be attributable to obesity, [. . .] the risk of death rises with increasing weight, [and] even moderate weight excess (10 to 20 pounds for a person of average height) increases the risk of death, particularly among adults aged 30 to 64 years, and [. . .] individuals who are obese (BMI > 30) have a 50 to 100% increased risk of premature death from all causes, compared to individuals with a healthy weight" ("Overweight and Obesity: Health Consequences," U.S. Department of Health and Human Services Web site). This data is controversial, as several recent well-done studies suggest that being moderately overweight may not be associated with excess mortality.

The specific conditions and illnesses that are associated with being overweight include cardiovascular disease, diabetes, cancer, respiratory problems, musculoskeletal conditions such as arthritis and joint problems, reproductive complications, urinary problems, and metabolic syndrome.

Health Risks of Obesity versus Risks of Weight-Loss Surgery

For some clients, the health risks of obesity and the difficulty of losing weight or maintaining a comfortable weight are so great that weight-loss surgery is recommended and undertaken. This decision should never be taken lightly and is an excellent topic to discuss in therapy. However, clients may be reluctant to bring up the issue for fear that the therapist will disapprove, judge them for "taking the easy way out," or try to dissuade them from going ahead with it. Although it is not our job to know everything about weight-loss surgery, it is important that we know the basics (at least as much as the client knows!) in order to converse intelligently on the subject.

Weight-Loss Surgery

Several procedures fall under this umbrella and are designed to produce weight loss by limiting the amount of food that can be eaten or absorbed. Current National Institutes of Health guidelines state that these surgeries are appropriate for people whose BMI is 40 or greater (about 100 pounds overweight) or for those who have a BMI of 35 with two or more significant obesity-related problems. The Weight Center at Massachusetts General Hospital and Harvard Medical Center maintains that "the risk of death due to bariatric surgery is below 1%, with about 10% of patients experiencing complications" (Tsao, 2004).

Mortality and complication rates depend on the procedure: In several large studies, the mortality rate associated with bariatric surgery was 0.1% to 2.0%. In a meta-analysis by Buchwald et al., operative mortality rates were 0.5% for gastric bypass, 0.1% for gastric banding, and 1.1% for malabsorptive procedures. (Bushwald, Avidor, Braunwald, Jensen, Pories, Fahrbach, Schoelles, 2004). Nonfatal perioperative complications include venous thromboembolism, anastomotic leaks, wound infections, bleeding, incidental splenectomy, incisional and internal hernias, and early small-bowel obstruction. In the Swedish Obesity Subjects trial, postoperative complications occurred in 13% of patients (DeMaria, 2007).

Outcome studies on improved health due to these surgeries vary and most are conducted for a mere 2-year period. Some of the research that has been conducted has been funded by surgery centers or companies that have a stake in study results. Clearly more long-term, unbiased studies are needed to understand what results are lasting and what complications may arise down the road.

Reviewing 136 studies on the results of weight-loss surgery, researchers found that it "reversed diabetes in 77% of obese patients, eliminated high blood pressure in 62%, and lowered cholesterol in at least 70%" (Taso, 2004). One study of 20,000 obese people in the United States and Sweden showed that "those who underwent surgery had a 30 to 40 percent lower risk of dying over the next seven to 10 years than those who went without the operations" (Stein, 2007).

However, another study involving about 1,200 Swedish people, half of whom had stomach-reducing surgery, found that initial numbers for such measurements as blood pressure, cholesterol, and blood sugar were vastly improved postsurgery but "within two years after the operation, any beneficial blood pressure and cholesterol effects were gone." Another study on postliposuction patients had similar conclusions (Kolata, 2007).

Gastric-Bypass Surgery and Gastroplasty

Bypass surgery, which is irreversible, reroutes the digestive system, which may lead to nutritional deficiencies that can cause severe health complications. Gastroplasty ("stomach stapling") does not involve "rerouting" and it is also irreversible. The only reversible procedure thus far is gastric banding. Potential side effects include "dumping syndrome," a combination of nausea, chest and abdominal cramps, sweating, and diarrhea, malabsorption of nutrients, vitamin deficiencies, and chronic abdominal pain. These symptoms are often avoided by eliminating foods that are high in sugar and fat from the diet. A rare, but possibly fatal, complication comes from leakage in the staple line.

Lap-Band

This procedure, which is reversible, creates a small pouch in the upper stomach that promotes feelings of fullness.

One obvious problem for the obese postsurgery is failure to engage in a more healthy lifestyle, which includes not only eating nutritiously and engaging in exercise, but reducing stress and getting sufficient sleep. Therapists treating clients who have had these surgeries need to help them monitor their health, especially in terms of negative surgical side effects. The medical community may want to play down these effects, fearing that too much discussion will drive patients away. However, clients need to be able to make informed decisions.

Although some clients go all out and make sufficient lifestyle changes to eat less and exercise more, many do not. They react similarly to those embarking on a diet—gung ho at the start followed by a decrease in motivation because modifying eating is so difficult. They may employ magical thinking along the lines of surgery "curing" their eating problems, or believe that they can continue to overeat or eat unhealthily because they have had the surgery. These clients require the same help and support that we give to people who have not had weight-loss surgery. Treatment needs to focus on why they make the food choices they do, ambivalence about weight reduction, and how to cope with difficult emotions without food.

— —

Liposuction

Also known as lipoplasty, liposuction is a body-shaping cosmetic surgery that removes fat from different body sites, including the abdomen, arms, thighs, neck, backs of arms, calves, face, and buttocks. Complications include allergic reactions to medications or surgical materials, infection, skin damage, contour irregularities, embolisms, and fluid imbalance. The best candidates have average or slightly above-average weight, have firm and elastic skin, are in good general health, and have pockets of fat that do not respond to reduction through diet and/or exercise.

At the other end of the spectrum from clients who seek out doctors to alter their insides or outsides are those who hate going to the doctor and avoid doing so, even when they are sick or have health problems. They may be fearful of hearing bad news or have had previous negative experiences with the medical community. This is especially true of clients who are excessively under- or overweight and suffer body shame and fear of how the health workers will react to their body size. Clients who are above or below average weight often complain of being lectured, talked down to, humiliated, and blamed for their medical problems by doctors, nurses, dieticians, physical therapists, and other health practitioners. Although some clients may be especially sensitive to being judged and may overreact to even the slightest criticism, there is good reason to believe that health professionals and paraprofessionals treat them differently because of their size.

Specifically, clients describe the following kinds of interactions. At times when they seek medical help for a specific problem, the practitioner makes the visit about eating and weight. This is especially true if clients are morbidly obese or grossly underweight. Clients are often so uncomfortable during the visit that they leave without being examined or having their health questions addressed. Moreover, if they later become acutely ill, they are less inclined to seek medical help and end up putting themselves at risk.

Clients also report being shamed about being too large or too thin, sometimes directly and sometimes in thinly veiled remarks made by medical personnel. This shame goes deep, to the point that some over- or underweight clients never look at their bodies, or catch a glimpse of themselves in a mirror and are repulsed. Being weighed at the outset of a doctor's visit is an extremely angst-ridden moment and some clients decline or refuse to step on the scale, only to be told that they must because it is "procedure." Underweight clients often prefer to be examined wearing at least some of their clothes because of their extreme discomfort being naked.

As clinicians, we may say that it is the client's shame that we need to deal with and that she need not feel it. Although this is partially true, it is also important for the health community to make facility visits (in the office, clinic, laboratory, and hospital) as comfortable as possible for all their patients and prioritize concerns such as whether it is more important to hear what a patient has to say and examine them or to weigh them. Generally, it is possible for medical staff to work around these issues, and their efforts go a long way toward helping over- or underweight clients become more at ease in these settings, which, in turn, encourages them to seek medical care when needed.

Overweight clients frequently describe being lectured about obesity, then given a diet plan to follow or a referral to a weight-loss program like Weight Watchers or Overeaters Anonymous to which they are encouraged to go. Although there may be some discussion about stressors in a patient's life causing overeating, she is not generally given a referral to a psychotherapist to help her cope more effectively. Underweight clients may even find themselves pushed toward eating disorder clinics and rehabilitation centers to force them to gain weight, and describe times when doctors refuse to treat them unless they comply. On the other hand, because anorexia nervosa is characterized by a high degree of denial, many clients who claim that they are naturally thin may have serious eating problems.

To assess the client's feelings about the medical/health profession, ask:

1. What are your general experiences with doctors and health practitioners?
2. What are your specific experiences with them regarding your weight or eating?
3. How concerned are you about the health risks of overeating/being overweight or undereating/being underweight?
4. What would make you more inclined to seek medical help (for instance, changing doctors, having a friend come along to appointments, preparing more for doctors' visits in therapy)?
5. How can I help make your experiences with the medical community go more smoothly?

Undoubtedly, most medical professionals are concerned about their patients' health and well-being. It is easy to understand how they come to feel helpless (as we often do) when they fail to see underfed patients gain weight or overweight ones lose it. It is not hard to appreciate their frustration when patients fall into denying, ignoring, or minimizing weight problems or become defensive as soon as the subject is raised. Practitioners know the life-threatening health risks for both populations and may see their patients as ticking time bombs. Believing that they have little or no impact on patients, they may give up or heavy-handedly pressure them to achieve or maintain a healthy weight. Many practitioners, unfortunately, fail to realize that building rapport with patients and creating a climate of trust, understanding, support, and good will goes a long way toward helping them share concerns and change behavior.

CHAPTER 5

Personality Traits and Family Dynamics

nyone can have eating and weight issues. For some clients, these problems are situational—postpregnancy, seeing a loved one through a terminal illness, or starting a stressful job—while others will tell you they cannot remember a time when they were not struggling with food or the scale. As discussed earlier, because of cultural stereotypes of fatness and thinness, it may be difficult *not* to think in terms of character traits for both of these groups. It is in our clients' interest, however, that we not only avoid pigeon-holing them because of their appearance or behaviors, but help them get out from under damaging stereotypes so that they may view themselves more clearly, objectively, wholly, and lovingly.

Although stereotypes remain largely untrue, there are certain aspects of personality that correlate with ongoing eating problems. Note, though, that this is an area in which we need to tread carefully to avoid blaming the victim. Because there is a substantial body of evidence that suggests that some 70% of our weight is genetically predetermined, we must make sure that we do not fault clients for something that is by and large out of their control (Kolata, 2007). The goal is to strike a balance between helping them recognize that no matter how hard they try, they will not be able to maintain a physiologically impossible weight, while encouraging them to do everything in their power to reach realistic eating and fitness goals (alas, no easy job!).

We also have to pay attention to cause and effect, that is, how having an eating or weight problem in childhood can shape or color a person's personality—how being a fat 4- or 5-year-old entering kindergarten might foster shyness, fear of rejection and exclusion, or the desire to please; how being a string bean among chunky siblings in a body-conscious family might generate guilt or fear of fat; how adolescent weight gain due to medication may increase insecurities about popularity and awkwardness in dating. The best way for practitioners to approach personality in relation to eating and weight is with an open mind that entertains all possibilities, the same way we endeavor to understand other issues that pertain to character development.

To understand how being over- or underweight affects the client, ask:

1. How has your weight affected your feelings about yourself during different times in your life?
2. How has being outside the norm influenced your attitude and behavior in terms of school, play, work, self-esteem, and socializing?
3. How has your body image shaped your personality and how have your personality traits impacted your body image?

Self-regulation

Patterns of over- and undereating (or alternating between the two) are often found in clients who have difficulty self-regulating in other areas of life as well. Whether the predominant cause of disregulation is bio-chemical or learned in the family (or, in all probability, a combination of the two) is yet to be learned. Most likely, appetite malfunction is a product of the intersection of nature and nurture, as heredity in the form of a neurotransmitter imbalance predisposes clients to disregula-tion and family interactions cement unhealthy behavioral responses. For instance, a child who is genetically inclined to put on weight will be reinforced by parents who cannot say not to food or by a food-centered extended family that celebrates cooking and feasting. This same child, raised by parents who attempt to eat healthily and stay fit or by a family that is not food-centered, may have less of a struggle managing appetite.

Self-regulation issues abound in our caseloads—clients are either too emotionally shut down or their lability and impulsivity make it dif-ficult for them to control emotional outbursts. They race through life as if the world will end tomorrow or stay in bed all day, are chronically late or compulsively on time, are shopaholics or mindlessly wear the same few outfits over and over. The list could go on and on chronicling addictions, phobias, and compulsions that drive clients to either over- or underdo. Practically speaking, most of us have regulatory difficul-ties in one area or another because that is the nature of being human. However, many clients have problems that make healthy functioning nearly impossible because they are riddled with chronic questions about what is enough.

Over time, treating clients with eating and weight issues, I have come to the conclusion that we should have a diagnostic classification called an Enough Disorder. Time and again, the same pattern emerges. A client cannot do enough to succeed at work or to help her friends and family, yet does little to take care of herself—perhaps other than eat. Or, a client cannot refrain from shopping because buy-ing new things gives him a high and saying no makes him feel deprived and depressed. More than any other, an Enough Disorder is a product of our times, when our historic Puritan ethic of self-denial collides with 21st-century materialism and overindulgence. We can ascribe some client difficulties in this area to cultural excess, but family and biology also play a large part in being unable to function within reasonable boundaries of "yes" and "no."

Knowing what is enough is described by Reindl (2001) as a *felt sense*, which is attributed to the realm of feeling because it registers as a ping of recognition, a thud of awareness. However, that does not mean that this felt sense emerges solely through sensation. Cognition plays a role, often unconscious, in this process as well, such as when we wonder if we are done with a task, tired and need to sleep, too busy to take a phone call, or crave time off or a vacation.

Recognizing what is enough is an idiosyncratic and fluid function. What is just right for one client is too much or too little for the next. Moreover, "enough" is not a static condition and what works to keep an individual in balance is strongly affected by external circumstances and changes over a life span. Self-regulation, therefore, involves not only knowing what is enough in any given moment, but being able to fluidly respond to the question correctly over and over, from moment to moment.

Many clients who have difficulty with states of hunger and satiation also struggle with other body issues. They do not know when it is time to rest or sleep, resisting bedtime (often staying up by eating) or using excessive sleep to reduce loneliness or boredom. They try repeatedly to fall asleep and rise at a sensible hour, only to slip out of the habit for no discernible reason and are unable to easily reestablish it. It seems as if their body has its own internal clock that is both arbitrary and capricious, sabotaging their best efforts to regulate sleep times and amounts.

Some clients run their bodies ragged until they are weak, sick, and exhausted, or cannot motivate themselves to do anything—chores, family commitments, socializing—for long periods of time. Or they begin a regimen of vitamin- or supplement-taking in an attempt to better care for their physical selves. Charging full speed ahead, they make detailed schedules of when to take what pill only to forget for a day, and leave the remainder of their supply forgotten in the refrigerator or medicine cabinet.

Such clients may also deal poorly with being unwell or in physical discomfort. They may either rush to the doctor at a hangnail or put off going with the oft-heard refrain of "I hate going to the doctor (or the hospital)," as if most people clamor at the chance. For the avoidant, forgotten are regular checkups and preventive care. These clients wait for their backs to be against the wall before seeking medical attention. Alternately, there are clients who spend their lives in doctors' waiting rooms, panicked at the smallest physical twinge, too anxious to ride out ailments, and fearful that something terrible will befall them if they do not nip conditions and diseases in the bud.

A sense of what the body needs in terms of activity and exercise can also become disregulated. How many times have we heard how wonderful clients feel when they sign up for a gym membership and go at regular intervals for a matter of days, weeks, or months? They swear they will never again stop exercising because their bodies feel so alive, so energized, so joyful at being active. Then, just when we believe they are finally committed to staying on track, they tell us that they missed a day or two at the gym or walking because they were sick, had out-of-town guests, or had been asked to work overtime. We watch helplessly as they suddenly or gradually give up exercise and fall into the same physical lethargy or passivity they were in before they started.

These types of disregulation that do not directly relate to appetite are important because they often do have a subtle to significant influence (depending on the client) on eating. For example, when clients fail to get sufficient sleep, they may become irritable, which may lead them to turn to food to soothe themselves. Or they may get so run down that they become ill and comfort or energize themselves with food treats. They might end up eating in order to stay up at night or fortify themselves with sustenance when they awaken exhausted in the morning or are ready to succumb to mid-afternoon fatigue.

From Chapter 3, it should be clear that appetite regulation, although considered a felt sense, is engineered from more than cognition and emotional awareness. Satiation and satisfaction in relation to food are primarily generated from leptin, ghrelin, and other hormones that influence hunger and fullness. Although we cannot know, unless clients are tested, whether they have an actual deficiency, glut, or imbalance of hormones, it is safe to assume that many of them suffer from appetite disregulation because their "appestat" is malfunctioning. Once again, clinicians have to be careful not to jump to the conclusion that only family dynamics, lack of insight, or insufficient motivation is at the root of disordered eating. In fact, it is likely that we will discover down the road that an imbalance of chemicals is responsible for many (if not most) kinds of disregulation and that these inequities drive a good deal of yes and no responses.

To assess the client's disregulation in areas other than eating and weight, ask:

1. Do you have trouble overdoing or underdoing, or often feel uncertain if enough is enough?
2. How do you decide whether something is sufficient, complete, or done?
3. Do you have difficulty regulating sleep, exercise, shopping, cleaning, or other activities?
4. Do you generally say yes to others and no to yourself or the other way around?

— —

Character traits

Many therapists already have an excellent sense of the character traits that accompany eating problems and disorders. Quite possibly, these qualities are precursors *to* eating issues rather than existing concurrently *with* them. Even when disordered eating is eliminated or, more realistically, decreased, clients continue to exhibit certain personality characteristics to greater or lesser extents. Fortunately, however, when inroads are made with food regulation, a client's personality may also change. For example, a client who has always considered herself on or off the diet bandwagon may, when more comfortable with food and at a reasonable weight, start to soften her all-or-nothing stance toward life. She may be able to find middle ground in areas such as sleep, social versus alone time, and time dedicated to others or self. A client who has never known satisfaction with food may gradually recognize sufficiency in other areas of life as he takes pride in knowing and respecting his limits, that is, if he can say no to food, he can refuse other things—stressful situations, intrusions, overdoing it at the gym, or excessive sexual activity.

One of the most obvious personality traits that permeates disordered eating is black-and-white or all-or-nothing thinking. In fact, as with addictions, it is a hallmark of eating dysfunction. Disordered eaters view the world in two camps—those who are fat and those who are thin, those who eat "normally" and themselves. Ask them to identify people they know who are of average weight or who seem comfortable around food, and they often have difficulty because *they fail to notice what is between either end of the eating or weight spectrum.* They will spout off the names of all the thin and fat eaters in their world, but "normal" eaters? And they do not polarize only in the weight arena; much of life is viewed in extremes of good or bad, on or off, in or out, easy or impossible.

All-or-nothing thinking in relation to food and body size is most dangerous in terms of either dieting or exerting no control over food choice or amount, in struggling to be thin or letting the pounds pile up until no-longer-thin becomes obese. When clients are at their slimmest, it is hard for them to imagine putting on so much weight that they would ever be considered fat. The same is true when they are at their highest weight and cannot entertain the possibility that they could ever lose enough weight to be happy and feel normal. Vaulting from one extreme to the other, they miss the middle ground, the center where they might be an average weight that does not preclude enjoyment of food but does involve ongoing self-monitoring.

Clients who are prone to black-and-white thinking may easily become addicted to dieting. No matter that they have lost and gained 100 pounds or more several times over, they are only able to conceive of their body in two ways: fat or slim. Therefore, when they are fat, the only answer is to diet and become thin. And if they cannot become as skinny as they desperately desire, why not simply shrug off all restraint and let themselves stay fat? They act as if they hear only two musical notes or see only two colors. It therefore falls to us to painstakingly point out every note on the scale and all the colors of the rainbow.

A good number of clients with eating problems suffer from a victim mentality. They are mired in the unfairness of and angry at the fact that they must struggle with food and the scale. Some believe they are powerless to reach their eating or weight goals and resent having to try so hard. They will tell you all the reasons they cannot stop overeating or start eating healthily—over-the-top job or family stress, co-workers or relatives who tempt them with goodies, friends who insist on socializing over food, a love of cooking, no time to shop for healthy foods—and all the situations that prevent them from exercising. They will insist that everyone in their family is fat, that they cannot fight genetics, so what's the point? They will try to convince you that it is too late to start getting healthy at 30 or 42 or 65 because the damage is already done. They will remind you of how many diets they have tried and failed at and how nothing has worked because they are simply too weak-willed or love food too much.

A victim mentality almost certainly dooms clients to failure, especially in tandem with all-or-nothing thinking. A client might lose some weight, but not all she wants or not as quickly as she would like—proof to herself that she really cannot have the body she wants—and give up. When success shoots holes in learned helplessness and challenges clients' self-view, they can become extremely uncomfortable. If they can learn to eat "normally" or reach a healthy weight, they will have to recognize that they have based their entire existence on a faulty premise, that is, they have wrongly believed they are victims of circumstance or have a black cloud hanging over their heads.

Another characteristic that is prevalent in clients who have eating and weight problems is denial and avoidance, or magical thinking. These ways of processing information are the same as those underlying addictive behaviors—change will happen without effort, no harm will come from self-destructive habits, the discomfort involved in changing patterns is unbearable and intolerable, and one can avoid having bad things happen if one refuses to think about them.

Anyone who has treated even a handful of clients knows the power of denial. Moreover, every therapist recognizes that this defense is universal and part of being human. Denial can be adaptive—think of the child who turns docile and quiet around a verbally abusive parent or the parent who maintains hope that a terminally ill child will recover—but it is a case of too much of a good thing. As we well know, clients who use denial habitually cannot help but cause themselves trouble and lead unhappy lives.

Nowhere is this truer than in dealing with eating and weight issues. Clients who have difficulty sitting with emotional discomfort or pain often use obsessing about food, preoccupation with thinness, or compulsive eating to ward off distress. They may truly believe that avoiding emotional discomfort is possible and in their best interest or that they are unable to bear painful affect. No matter what they believe; we know that they will end up trading unfamiliar emotional upset for the self-hate and contempt that will surely come after overeating. For example, a client who is fired from his job might find it too upsetting to contemplate his work history or future. Instead, he eats. What he refuses to acknowledge is that his denial will inevitably lead to more pain—when his clothes are too tight or, still jobless, when he is evicted for not paying his rent.

Magical thinking plays such an overwhelming part in eating and weight problems that it needs to be thought of as a special kind of denial, functioning on many levels. It is there when a client eats mostly junk food and does not think about her health, when she says she will start her diet tomorrow or the next day or after the wedding or on New Year's Day, when she cannot fit into her clothes and blames the problem on dryer shrinkage, when she has downed a box of cookies but fools herself into believing that it is okay because they are low fat. Magical thinking operates on so many levels in weight and eating disorders—from the physical aspect of eating to considering its consequences—that we can almost say that a client who ceases magical thinking might cease to struggle with eating.

To help the client understand how specific personality traits influence eating and weight problems, ask:

1. Do you tend to view the world in black-and-white or all-or-nothing terms?
2. What role does denial or magical thinking play in your food and weight problems?

3. Does difficulty experiencing uncomfortable emotions play a part in your food abuse?
4. Are you a pessimist or an optimist and how does your outlook on life affect your eating difficulties?

Another characterological issue that underlies eating problems involves internal conflict about dependence. For clients who have difficulty being independent and autonomous, food is the perfect crutch. It is always there and never demands a thing in return. Rather than working on increasing ego strength, clients instead fall into the trap of depending on food to lift them over life's rough spots. Rather than learning to speak up and assert their needs, set goals and persevere, or find meaning through work or creativity, they rely on a narrow dependence on food. They eat to quash feelings, to soothe themselves, for something to do, to arouse passion, and to give meaning to life (that is, they live to eat).

Other clients, a substantial number with food problems, are counterdependent. In childhood, they learned that they could not readily depend on people or their own internal resources to meet their emotional needs, and they eventually buried or spurned these authentic desires. These clients insist that they value independence over dependence, yet what they yearn for more deeply than anything— more than ice cream and chocolate, even—are understanding, connection, support, companionship, comfort, and validation, things only another human can provide.

One of the problems with attempting to be completely autonomous and not rely on people emotionally is that it is highly stressful, causing more of a need to depend and exacerbating a vicious cycle. The more strongly counterdependent clients feel a need for other people, the greater their denial or suppression of this unwanted yearning, and the more likely they are to turn to food. When clients equate mental health and emotional well-being with total self-sufficiency, they are cutting off half their emotional selves. The more pronounced this personality feature, the more difficulty clients have regulating their eating and, ultimately, their weight.

More often than not, a harsh superego and a tendency toward perfectionism are characteristics of people who have eating or weight problems. This is especially true of chronic undereaters and those who are underweight. They want desperately to be perfect (it may be their unspoken supreme and only goal) and that means having the ideal body. No matter that they come from a line of short, heavyset ancestors or have a terrible sweet tooth and hate vegetables or have been chubby since childhood. This desire for body perfection overwhelms reality and objectivity and can drive clients into relentlessly endangering their health.

However, people who are overweight and overeaters also may have a proclivity toward perfection. Ironically, it is often the case that the only place they allow themselves to be imperfect is around food. We know that everyone must be able to tolerate creating a mess, making mistakes, and failing. Clients who are overachievers and who try to live up to unrealistically high standards often find that the only place they can "let it all hang out" and not hold themselves on such a tight leash is with food. The more they try to achieve, succeed, and be faultless and flawless in other areas of life, the more out of control their eating becomes.

Clients who are perfectionists are really afraid of failure, making mistakes, and feeling ashamed. They are driven to do well so that they do not have to feel the shame that lurks close to the surface. Shame of this kind is due to growing up in shame-based families that could not teach them how to bear feelings of inadequacy and incompetence. However, because emotions will do their darndest to get us to attend to them, shame cannot help but emerge—for these clients, in the realm of eating and weight. When a client struggles with shame, there will always be some behavior in her life, some tell, that leads her back to that emotion.

A sister characteristic to perfectionism is when clients are exceedingly hard on themselves and possess only a minimum of self-compassion. More often than not, these clients are overly compassionate with others, but not always; sometimes they are, indeed, hard task masters and their standards are unreasonably lofty all around. Failing to recognize that the carrot often works better than the stick, their fear is that unleashing self-understanding will lead to having no standards at all. Perfectionism and a harsh superego are a powerful duo, and keep the disordered eater in a rat race of trying harder and harder to succeed. Because they interpret every failure at curbing appetite or losing weight as as a result of their ineffectiveness, they redouble their efforts in order to keep shame at bay.

Clients who regularly sabotage their best efforts to eat well and lose weight also tend to harbor underlying, unconscious mixed feelings about being thin and fat. Again, this is not true of all over-weight clients, due to the fact that some may be trying to dip below their set point. But those who have internal conflicts about weight often play them out through self-sabotage. For some, the conflict revolves around deservedness. As they approach their target weight, they unconsciously recoil in doubt about whether they are worthy of being happy and healthy. Another inner tug-of-war is what it means to be thin: Will they be hit on more romantically or sexu-ally? What if life still is not perfect? What if they feel too good about themselves? Clients often fear that once they are thin they will have to give up enjoying food forever, and most have valid mis-givings about doing so.

Additionally, sabotage might occur if clients are conflicted about an unhappy relationship or situation—if they feel better about themselves, might they leave an unlovable or mismatched spouse or a partner? Will looking better move them closer to quitting a job they hate and throw them out into a tight employment market? If they feel fit and in control, will they move away from parents or siblings who have an unhealthy investment in their sticking around? We cannot help clients when they sabotage themselves over and over if we are unable to help them decode what this start-and-stop behavior means, if we are unable to untangle competing fears and desires that, unresolved, will always bring clients back to the status quo.

Another area that presents difficulties for overeaters and under-eaters relates closely to self-regulation: setting and keeping boundaries. Clients with eating issues are inclined to be what might be termed porous, that is, they empathize strongly and overidentify to the point of taking on others' pain. They are therefore often the kinds of people who will give you the shirt off their back. All well and good, we might say as therapists, if you have other shirts. But, often, these clients metaphorically do not. What they have is an enormous difficulty setting tight, safe, secure boundaries around themselves so that they will not be hurt or taken advantage of. Their boundaries are, instead, loose and wide open, which generally lets in trouble.

To help the client understand how specific personality traits influence eating and weight problems, ask:

1. Is it easier to depend on food for comfort or excitement than people? Why?
2. How does your ability or inability to set and keep boundaries affect your eating?
3. Do you strive to be perfect? What happens when you are not?
4. What do you fear about failure and making mistakes?

> 5. Do you often feel shame about your thoughts or actions?
> 6. Do you sabotage your best efforts at eating and losing weight? Why?

There is a final set of traits, which Freud labeled emotional defenses, that are employed frequently by clients with eating and weight problems. Denial, avoidance, and magical thinking have already been discussed, but other less prominent defenses also plague this population. One is *rationalizing*, which occurs when clients, in the moment, entertain the belief that overeating is not going to make a big difference in their weight—just a honey-glazed doughnut here, an extra Snickers bar there. Clients may also *minimize* strengths and accomplishments, shrinking them to almost nonexistent in comparison to their mistakes and failures. They focus on the weight they have yet to lose rather than what already has come off, ignore their amazing achievements, and zero in on being out of control around food or the plus-size dress they are wearing.

Projection is another defense that is often part of the overeaters' arsenal. They tend to ascribe their own intensely negative feelings about fatness and positive feelings about thinness to other people. This is not to say that we do not live in a fat-phobic culture. We most assuredly do, and as therapists we must acknowledge that overweight clients go out every day of their lives and have to work and play in a thin-is-in world.

However, it is not true that everyone a fat person comes in contact with will think badly of or feel contempt for them. People may harbor unkind thoughts, but few will express them. In fact, for the most part, clients have no idea what folks think of their size. Perhaps, because they do not know or cannot imagine anyone accepting or feeling compassion for being oversized, they assume something negative. That way, of course, they are at least prepared if someone judges them harshly. However, this kind of thinking also sets them up to expect and assume the worst, which works against building self-confidence and self-esteem.

To help the client evaluate use of unhealthy emotional defenses that may work against achieving eating and weight goals, ask:

1. Do you minimize your strengths and often focus on your weaknesses or challenges?
2. How does rationalizing get you into trouble with abusing food?
3. Do you feel so negative about your body that you assume other people will as well?
4. Are you always expecting and girding yourself for the worst?

Although eating disorders and problems can be found across every Axis II diagnosis, they are more prevalent in some than others. A detailed discussion of food problems and Axis I diagnoses such as anxiety, dissociative disorders, and depressive disorders may be found in Chapter 7, "Clinical Disorders."

Because three of the key criteria for borderline personality disorder (BPD) are affective instability, impulsivity, and chronic feelings of emptiness, it is often linked to eating problems. Although many people with disordered eating cannot tolerate intense affect, are impulsive, and eat to fill up an internal emptiness, not every disordered eater has BPD. However, especially in cases of intractable bulimia and anorexia, this diagnosis should be seriously considered.

Affective instability, often called lability, occurs when clients rapidly move from one mood or state of mind to another. They describe feeling ruled by shifting moods and unable to regulate intensity. This difficulty is likely due to an imbalance in neurotransmitters that modulate affect, but may also be rooted in a history of trauma and in a family situation in which parents were unable to soothe themselves or the client. The client with BPD, therefore, often feels at the mercy of her emotions and is at a complete loss of what to do with them. Unfortunately, abusing food (overeating or obsessing about weight and calories) often acts as a soothing agent and becomes a learned way for these clients to contain their feelings.

Because they are impulsive, clients with BPD are at high risk in many areas for acting first and thinking later. They often understand that they act rashly but feel powerless to stop themselves. It is unclear whether they have learned to bypass using good judgment or whether their impulses are so powerful that their frontal lobes cannot kick into gear quickly enough to control behavior. Clients who eat impulsively often feel terrible regret and fear (of gaining weight) *after* a food abuse incident. The goal is to help them move this fear ahead of their behavior so that they can predict its consequence.

Feelings of chronic emptiness seduce clients with BPD into trying to fill themselves up with material things, substances, achievement, or busyness. Again, studies suggest that there is a biological component to "the hole" described by these clients that is based on imbalanced neurotransmitters. It is likely, again, that at least some of these clients have a genetic tendency toward feeling empty and that, in childhood, they did not learn effective ways to feel filled up. Food is so accessible that we can see how it becomes easy pickings for someone who cannot tolerate an inner void.

Another Axis II diagnosis that is often found in people with eating problems is avoidant personality disorder (APD). Key criteria include fear of engaging in relationships and discomfort in social situations. Lacking companionship and deep emotional attachments, clients with APD may view food as a best friend who will never reject or ridicule them. We might not realize that clients have APD until we fully understand how they function in intimate relationships and social situations. A tip-off is a client who has few, if any, close friends. When we ask about friendships, we might find our client indifferent to intimacy. Sometimes a client with APD is far more comfortable with animals than people, and may have several or a string of pets. She may appear a loner by choice, and it may take a long time to understand the depth and breadth of rejection and/or abandonment that makes her feel so uncomfortable in relationships with people.

This kind of client goes out of her way to not place herself in settings in which there are a great many people. She might say she is too busy to attend an after-work party or that she cannot possibly make her cousin's wedding because it is too far to travel. What she is not saying is how awkward and frightened she feels at gatherings and how heightened internal distress keeps her away from them. Fear of intimacy and of social situations is a setup for clients with APD who have eating problems. Because they have no, or few, close friends to share upset with, they may turn to food for comfort. And because they avoid social activities, they are often alone with too much time on their hands; eating becomes a low-anxiety activity that is always within reach.

Clients who have dependent personality disorder (DPD), characterized by discomfort at being alone and exaggerated fears of being unable to care for themselves, are also at risk for food-related problems. For them, food is a way to nurture, comfort, and soothe themselves and make them feel less alone. In a way, they have the opposite set of issues from the client with APD, because their anxiety derives from being alone. They therefore seek out other people 24/7 and when they are alone, their anxiety is so high that the turn to food to for self-soothing.

These clients do not believe that they can take care of themselves, whether they appear to have the skills or not (and generally they do

not). Because they do not know many non-food ways to nurture themselves, food becomes the universal panacea. Regularly turning to food
for self-care in turn precludes them from developing more effective
and appropriate strategies and reinforces their belief that they are
unable to adequately take care of themselves.

To assess whether the client may have an underlying character disorder that contributes to eating and weight problems, ask:

1. Do you have problems controlling your impulses, feel
   empty inside a lot, or have shifting moods that seem to
   come out of nowhere?
2. How do you feel about being close with people and about
   engaging in social situations? Does your anxiety go up or
   down around people?
3. What do you think of your ability to take care of yourself
   compared to other people's ability to care for you? Are
   you more comfortable around people or alone?

Family dynamics can also be a major contributor to eating and
weight problems. Obviously, for a young child or adolescent, how her
parents regulate her food consumption and the eating behavior they
model will be the largest factors, other than genetics, affecting her
relationship with food and her body. Parents who are "normal" eaters
and have a healthy attitude toward weight will likely produce children
who are comfortable in their bodies and around food.

On the other hand, parents who are uptight around food—
obsessed with calorie- and fat-gram counting, constantly dieting or
monitoring their food intake, or who eschew anything but "health
foods"—pass along to their children distorted, negative messages

about the positive role food should play in life. Moms and dads who regularly struggle with their children around food issues, especially if they try to rigidly control what gets eaten (or not eaten), are setting the stage for future eating dysfunction. At the other end of the spectrum, parents who pay no attention to nutrition and make a habit of emotional or compulsive eating are also programming their children to neither feed their bodies nor manage their feelings effectively.

The act of feeding is not the only behavior that leaves an imprint on children's attitudes toward food and weight. Parents who are preoccupied with their own, their partner's, or their children's weights are modeling a mind-set that says there is not a range of acceptable weights, only one ideal number for each person, which implies that there is something wrong if a body does not achieve it. Clients who grow up with parents who overtly or covertly express extreme dissatisfaction with their own or each other's bodies pick up the attitude that bodies cannot be loved unconditionally, but must be whipped into acceptability. Children also suffer enormously when their young, growing bodies are criticized and when parents overfocus on weight, whether it is above or below normal. Moreover, parents who are always talking about eating, exercise, and weight loss make it seem as if this is natural and normal, and overemphasize the importance of food and fitness to being happy and successful.

Comments do not have to be directed at the client to leave their mark. Family members who make frequent pronouncements about fat or thin people in public or in the family or who make a habit of criticizing or praising each other's weight give children the impression that it is natural and acceptable to be judgmental about body size and shape. Most damaging is hearing one parent constantly chastise or demean the other for what she weighs or eats. Even if the child is not the target of remarks, he learns that it is the norm to make harsh judgments about what a person eats or weighs.

Criticism can be especially devastating when children reach

puberty and have to deal with a host of physical changes. If parents are relaxed about these changes and explain them as natural, children become comfortable with their bodies. When parents ignore these transformations or are frightened by them, teenagers may believe that their shifting shapes are abnormal and scary. Additionally, parents who make no effort to be fit and maintain a healthy weight are setting the stage for their children to let themselves go and not take care of their bodies.

Family dynamics do not stop affecting clients' views about food and their bodies when clients reach adulthood, especially under two conditions. The first is when clients have not adequately separated emotionally from parents and are unable to think for themselves about (and stand up for) their size and how they wish to eat. The second is when parents—or other family relatives—violate boundaries and comment on clients' eating and weight. Family remarks are frequently triggers for acting out with food, whether what is said is positive or negative or intended as helpful or hurtful.

To assess how upbringing might affect the client's attitude toward food and their body, ask:

1. How would you describe your parents' attitude toward food and eating when you were growing up?
2. How would you describe their attitude about weight?
3. What family messages make it especially hard to have a positive relationship with food?
4. What family messages make it difficult to feel good about your body at any weight?
5. What family relationships today influence how you feel about food and your body?
6. How can I help you improve those relationships?

Although some disordered eaters might be substantially free of character disorder, most were raised in families in which messages about food and body size were unhealthy, and these are the messages clients are carrying around today. By helping clients evaluate how their personality impacts their eating and weight problems, we give them a chance to change their attitudes and beliefs. By helping them understand how family dynamics shaped their mind-set about food and body, we give them a chance to overcome learned dysfunction and move toward healing.

CHAPTER 6

Assessment

An initial therapeutic assessment of clients usually falls into one of three categories: we know very little, if anything, about the client, and therefore all of the (verbal and nonverbal) information they give us is new; we have a sketchy idea of what is going on from an intake, referral source, family member, or brief phone conversation; or we have received an extensive verbal or written history about the client and have a clear idea what to expect before we even say hello.

Although it generally takes a few appointments to gather a thorough family history and numerous sessions to deeply understand clients' interpersonal and intrapsychic issues, one thing we cannot help but see at a first meeting is a client's weight. We may be tempted to make assumptions, but we should refrain. If the clients are underweight, there is little way of knowing whether they are unable to keep on pounds, diet to stay thin, are naturally slim, are highly athletic or active, or yo-yo wildly between weights every few months or years. Further, we cannot be certain what kind of eaters they are based on their size. They may eat normally, binge and purge, weigh every morsel that enters their mouth, or eat junk food but exercise excessively.

If clients are heavy, we also have no way of ascertaining how being overweight affects them either physically or emotionally. Is weight gain recent or have they been large their whole lives; are they fat, fit, and healthy, or is their being overweight part of a larger self-care issue; did they try dieting once and give up or have they spent a lifetime going from one weight-loss program to another in vain; is this the thinnest or fattest they have ever been or somewhere in between?

It is difficult not to make assumptions when clients are overweight or obese. We may naturally assume that a heavy client hates herself or that a skinny one feels great about her body. Moreover, we need to guard against projecting our own (often unconscious) feelings about body size onto the client—one way or the other. It is easy to make a snap judgment that a client does not care how she looks or jump to the conclusion that a stout client is not fit or does not eat healthily. The truth may be that she engages in regular exercise, eats a vegan diet, and is large-boned, all muscle and fit as a fiddle.

Some clients who weigh less than the norm are happy about it, some would not mind putting on a few pounds but simply are not that interested in food, and others rarely think about weight one way or the other. That said, it would not be unusual for a clinician to assume that an underweight client is happy with her size and that an overweight client is unhappy. That might even be true. But the fact is that we do not know what meaning, if any, weight has to the client until we observe or receive some direct or indirect communication that affirms or challenges our hunches.

Our job is to help clients open up about their problems, then guide them toward resolving them. Whether they suffer under an abusive boss, have suddenly lost a spouse, or are recovering from PTSD, we must listen to everything they have to say—along with how they say it—and determine what is vital from what is not. During this process, we are naturally tuning in to some things and not others, automatically prioritizing what is important to therapy and what seems incidental, what needs addressing now and what can be kept on the back burner until later. We are involved in an inevitable and necessary—conscious and unconscious—selection process that gets therapy moving and keeps it going in a constructive direction.

Unfortunately, unless we are tuned in to them, eating and weight issues may get lost in the therapeutic shuffle as we try to help clients work through crises, overcome troubled or traumatic pasts, and grapple with challenging, uncertain futures. We may consider a client's worries about weight gain from a pregnancy trivial compared to her infant being born with Down's syndrome, minimize another's complaints about losing her appetite due to postmastectomy chemotherapy in favor of talking about how the surgery affects her femininity, or fail to pick up on a divorcé's lament that all he wants to do is watch TV and eat junk food since his wife walked out on him. Client problems may be so life-threatening or overwhelming that not only do we fail to attend to less significant issues, but end up ignoring them altogether as we attempt to steer clients out of danger and onto safer ground or avoid backsliding.

In all these instances, there are what we may call major and minor themes to the therapy: A Down's syndrome infant, mastectomy, and divorce may all be considered "major," while gaining weight, loss of appetite, and becoming a junk-food junkie in and of themselves may be viewed as "minor." Major themes are of immediate concern and involve strong emotions or serious repercussions; minor themes appear less consequential and fail to carry intense affect. What we make of and how we attend to both categories is what shapes the therapy from our end. The better we are at picking up, sorting out, prioritizing, and integrating all the information we have about the client, the greater the chance that we can help them achieve *all* of their (stated and unstated) goals.

My point is to underscore that just because eating and/or weight concerns arise in conjunction with other problems—or lurk in their shadows—does not mean that they are not legitimate and pressing. Along with including relevant comments about food or weight in our clinical notes, we need to acknowledge and validate client concerns, or mention that we would like to return to these issues down the road. At the very least, we must convey that we heard their words, registered their feelings, and are open to exploring them. A client may not even realize how worries about food and weight gradually become therapeutic themes. One client may be unaware that in every session she alludes to a fear of getting fat; another may not recognize that every appointment begins with a recitation of how much he has overeaten during the past week.

Reflections for Therapist

1. How do you arrive at conclusions regarding how clients relate to food and their bodies?
2. Do you generally have a good idea of how clients feel about eating and weight?
3. Have you ignored or overlooked clients mentioning these issues?
4. What questions could you ask that would give you a fuller picture?
5. How ready is the client to discuss and work on these issues? How ready are you?

After we have some idea of clients' views on food and feelings about their bodies, it is time to share our assessment or thoughts and, perhaps, even to give feedback. As the saying goes, timing is all—although there is no perfect moment to bring up an issue, *when* we offer our perspective does matter and is as important as *what* we have to say. Experienced clinicians often intuit when the moment feels right, when clients appear most open—or least closed—to hearing an analysis of their problems, but even seasoned practitioners may end up voicing their opinions to deaf ears when denial, avoidance, deflection, and conflicting feelings come into play.

One way to assess a client's feelings in the food and body arenas is to raise questions as part of the initial interview, when much ground is covered across a wide spectrum of issues. An excellent assessment survey—which touches not only on food but on related issues—can be found online at www.aplaceofhope.com. Briefer questionnaires can be found at www.healthybodyimage.com and www.counseling.gmu.edu. These tools will help both clinician and client identify the nature and extent of eating problems. The therapist can employ them as part of a wider assessment and get more information as the therapy moves along or use them to address these issues in the moment.

To understand the importance of the client's eating and weight concerns, ask:

1. How significant are your eating, weight, and body image concerns compared to other problems in your life?
2. Do other people think they are more or less important than you do?
3. How important are they now compared to the past? Why is that?
4. How crucial is their resolution to meeting your life goals?

These questions will aid therapist and client in putting the subject into perspective and help them reflect on the value of further discussion. If the clinician is lucky, a client might raise food or body image concerns at the start of therapy when she is setting therapeutic goals. However, merely because she identifies weight loss or stopping dieting and eating "normally" as a goal does not mean that she will not have mixed feelings about doing so. As with other goals, we must assist a client in examining what will help and hinder her from reaching eating and weight objectives, how she will overcome obstacles, and how conflicting or mixed emotions about success and failure may undermine or sabotage her best efforts.

Many clients do not have severe enough disorders to fit into diagnostic categories. Others dislike having a clinical label slapped on their behavior and may minimize problems so that they sound less serious and dysfunctional. More likely, clients will think of themselves as under- or overeaters, chronic dieters or restrictive, emotional or compulsive eaters. They may say things like, "I eat too much, I'm an emotional eater, I'm always on a diet, I'm always trying to lose weight, I'm not all that interested in food." Most will make a connection between elevated weight and what or how much they eat, but some will not and, instead, will view their weight issues as separate from their eating habits. In rare cases this may be true for clients who are on medications or who have hormonal or medical issues that cause weight gain or loss.

It is helpful to keep in mind that although a client may seem desperate to increase or decrease her weight or to change her eating habits, she may harbor a slew of unconscious feelings that could prevent or impede progress. It is tempting but imprudent to take at face value a client's stated desire to exercise more, eat healthily, go on a diet, curb emotional eating, or stop restricting her food intake. It is fine to consider these desires as manifest goals as long as latent goals are explored as well. Unfortunately, *it is common for a client to be totally out of touch with fears of losing or gaining weight, giving up food as comfort, or using a food obsession to mask other life problems.* For example, a client who promises herself to get to the gym more often may not recognize that she is terrified of losing weight and being viewed as a sexual object. Another who appears gung ho about overcoming his use of laxatives may not realize how frightened he is of becoming as fat as he was in childhood, when his family severely restricted his food intake and his classmates taunted him daily.

Because our role is part cheerleader, it is difficult not to get attached to clients' goals of losing or gaining weight or overcoming eating problems, especially when we understand how unhappy they are. We must use therapy to keep them motivated—pointing out their progress and praising them for a job well done—while remaining relatively unattached to outcomes, a tough job indeed. In discussing these subjects, we must always focus on how the client can motivate himself and what underlying and possibly unconscious issues might get in his way. We may be rooting for clients inside, and even let them know that we think they are doing a terrific job, but we should avoid the trap that diet counselors, coaches, and programs fall into by supporting only their hopes and not exploring their fears.

To assess the client's motivation to change eating habits, ask:

1. Have you tried to change your eating before? How did that work out?
2. What prevented you from changing your eating permanently? What prevented you from reaching or maintaining weight goals?
3. Is anything different now that will make success more possible?
4. What do you think will prevent you from reaching your eating and weight goals?

Another trap that can ensnare us is feeling obligated to offer nutritional and exercise advice. This approach occurs when we have the mistaken view that all a client needs is more information about how to lose weight, and off he will go and do it. With the medical community and the media's constant onslaught of facts about disease and mortality and tips on how to eat right, it makes sense that we belive that nutritional knowledge will lead to a healthy weight. *The truth is that many people already know the basics of nutrition.* How can they not? We are bombarded daily with food facts and messages about the benefits of weight loss and exercise. Unless we have a dual degree as a psychotherapist and a registered dietician or physical education expert, we need to go easy on dispensing advice and suggestions. Far better to work our psychological magic and let nutritionists and trainers do their jobs.

Reflections for Therapist

1. Is asking about eating and weight part of your usual assessment or intake process?
2. If not, how do you gather information about these areas?
3. Do you regularly ask about weight and medical history for family members?
4. Do you regularly ask about food, body image, and weight issues when collecting information about the client's childhood?

Doing an assessment of clients' eating and weight concerns may be an easy or difficult task. Clients may tell you right off the bat that they have been in rehab for bulimia or have been dieting and recently lost 40 pounds. On the other hand, they may talk about everything but their food problems and even deny having them. As with other issues, our job is to peel back the layers gradually and create a safe environment for clients to comfortably share concerns.

There are several ways that clients approach these issues that are worth bearing in mind. In general, it is more likely that an overweight (than an underweight) client will acknowledge eating and weight problems in order to get help. Although she may minimize overeating, binge eating, eating in secret, hoarding food, or having health, work, or intimacy problems, she will usually admit to some concerns. As she finds that she can speak openly without being judged or lectured, she will probably become increasingly honest. The more accepting we are of her eating and weight problems, the more she will be able to tell us how badly they plague her.

Underweight clients, on the other hand, are more likely to ignore or deny low weight or undereating, even if it is a problem. Their attitude is understandable when we consider how highly prized being thin is—no matter how a client gets there, she may not want to give up living out an ideal. How can she help but be aware that mentioning food restriction, weight obsession, purging, overexercising, or a desire to binge will eventually lead her down the path of facing and possibly giving up her unhealthy habits? Moreover, although overweight clients occasionally may be coerced into therapy by relatives, they often enter from their own volition and on some level want to become healthier.

This is not necessarily true of clients who enjoy being ultraslim. Many end up in therapy due to pressure from others and strongly may prefer not to be in treatment. They may only be sitting before us because it is the lesser of two evils (that is, therapy is required in an aftercare plan, parental insistence that a child living at home go for counseling, a spouse or partner threatening to dissolve the relationship if the client does not get help, etc.). In these cases, try to understand two things. First, the client may adamantly refuse therapeutic efforts to engage because she is panicked that her eating behavior, her way of coping with everyday stresses and pressures to be thin, will be taken away. Second, she may push away attempts to reach out to her and still want help because she is scared of harming herself through food abuse.

Many underweight clients are in outright denial, which is readily apparent when the therapist runs through the list of health hazards that result from anorexia, bulimia, overexercising, and/or rigidly restricting food intake and the client either refuses to acknowledge their existence, minimizes their severity, rationalizes them away, or changes the subject. Although overweight clients may also downplay the medical risks of excess pounds, it is sometimes easier for them to admit their concerns because of how the media has played them up. Moreover, they probably have heard the same comments about health risks from multiple sources—doctors, friends, family, co-workers. Underweight clients, on the other hand, often hear praise for their thinness and get cultural (even medical) validation for their restrictive eating and preoccupation with staying slim.

At the other end of the spectrum are clients who come into sessions and overfocus on eating and weight. Rather than talk about relationship difficulties or work dilemmas, their conversations always center around food and the scale. If we let them, they would spend every minute of every session detailing what they have eaten or not eaten. They would bring in food and weight logs, explain in detail their diet plan, and even ask the therapist to read the book that describes their weight-loss program. They would describe their exercise schedule and routine, explain the benefits of macrobiotic eating, or chronicle their weight-loss efforts over the past few decades (not to be confused with giving an appropriate weight history).

These "overfocused" clients truly believe that talking about their eating and weight problems to the exclusion of every other life issue will help them reach their goals. Most will not recognize that using up therapy time talking about these issues is a way of distancing themselves from underlying ones that need to be addressed to eat "normally." Clients who are preoccupied with weight—losing or gaining—often are addicted to the process itself as a way to cope and keep anxiety about many other aspects of life at bay.

Two of the major reasons that clients fail to raise concerns about food and the scale are shame and fear of being humiliated. They may be unaware that they are embarrassed about their eating behaviors or that they fear being shamed if they bring them up. Some clients will shift subjects the moment the therapist hints at food or weight problems. Others will acknowledge having issues, but tell you that they are working on them and do not need help. Still others will engage in superficial chitchat on the subject or discuss goal setting without really sharing their deepest fears and feelings about being fat or thin, eating with too much or too little control, or how desperate and depressed they are as they struggle with their bodies.

It is helpful to assess how much shame clients appear to have before moving too quickly into the food and weight arenas. Can they tolerate talking about being teased as a child for being fat? Talk openly about sexual problems with a partner that are due to obesity? Are they comfortable looking in the mirror and being honest about their food intake? Some clients are so ashamed of what they perceive as their gluttony or secret eating that they will lie or avoid mentioning these behaviors. If we are not tuned into the intense shame that runs beneath the surface of most eating and weight problems, we may take what the client says at face value without realizing what is being covered up.

To assess how the client feels about eating and weight, ask:

1. Are you satisfied with your weight? If not, why not?
2. Are you satisfied with your relationship with food? If not, why not?

3. Have you talked about eating or weight problems with other people? If not, why not?
4. Is there any reason you might be uncomfortable talking about these subjects?
5. How do you expect me to react when you bring them up?
6. How would you like me to react when you bring them up?

Clients feel bad about food and weight problems for a number of reasons. Many were overweight children who were teased by family members, friends, and classmates. Whether teasing was meant good-naturedly or not, it still stung. They may have extreme sensitivity when discussing body issues, even when we are trying to alleviate and eliminate shame in the long run. Other clients are less embarrassed about weight than eating—the fact that they barely eat enough to survive, that they have been in and out of rehab for years and still purge, that they lack "willpower," that they engage in wild food binges that leave them exhausted and filled with self-loathing, that they have dieted most of their life or have had bariatric surgery and are still fat.

Clients also feel shame because people have ignored their pleas for help, castigated them for not being disciplined around food, or made food and weight a huge issue. Generally, if overweight clients are surrounded by friends and family who love and respect them, their shame will be less than if their "loved ones" are constantly on them to get or stay thin. Moreover, they may have encountered folks in the helping professions who have been less than kind about their weight, who have harshly lectured them about obesity and health risks, or who have shoved a diet plan at them, but given them no real understanding, encouragement, or support.

Many clients come to therapy having been in previous treatment.

Depending on their experience in general as well as their specific encounters about eating and weight, they will be more or less open about their problems. Many clients have tried to work on food issues in therapy only to find clinicians ignorant, uninterested, unhelpful, and unresponsive at best—and derisive at worst. Therapists may joke about these topics, sweep them under the rug, or even deride clients for being obsessed about losing weight or maintaining thinness. In most circumstances, clients have been working on other issues and may have only mentioned food concerns in passing; in other situations, clients have made valiant efforts to raise their difficulties, to no avail.

When clients believe their needs are going unheard or being ignored, they may not understand that this is the fault of the therapist. Sometimes, due to lack of education on the subject or conflicted emotions and negative countertransference, we shy way from talking about eating and weight issues. Unfortunately, clients generally fail to recognize that *we* are the ones having a tough time with the subject and, instead, feel ashamed for burdening us therapists with a difficult or onerous problem. They may internalize our projection of shame about our own bodies or our helplessness at not knowing how to resolve their problems.

Often clients pick up on the shame that we feel about commenting on their weight. Perhaps an obese client has difficulty finding a comfortable office chair or enters the session huffing and puffing from climbing a flight of stairs. Being kind-hearted souls, we frequently go out of our way to avoid making clients uncomfortable, so that instead of remarking how difficult it must be to find a chair or remarking on someone being out of breath, we say nothing. If clients encounter this kind of reaction repeatedly, they may interpret our silence as our desire to avoid talking about their weight problem because it makes *us* uncomfortable. That is, instead of allowing us to take care of them, they end up trying to take care of us at their own expense.

Even if a therapist is not nearly ready to make a comment or ask a question about body size after noting that weight seems to be a physical problem for a client—and most therapists would not feel at ease until after a few sessions—observing how clients move, where they choose to sit, how they get comfortable, and how they hold their body may give valuable assessment clues. Some clients look as if they are trying hard not to take up too much space, while others appear to enjoy spreading out and claiming space as their own. Some carry themselves with great dignity and grace, while others look as if they would like to hide or disappear.

To assess the client's feelings about discussing weight and eating issues, ask:

1. Are you comfortable talking about eating and weight issues with me? If not, what could I do to make you more at ease?
2. Do you feel shame about your eating or weight? If so, why?
3. How have other therapists treated your food or body concerns?
4. How have other health professionals treated them?
5. What are your fears or doubts about discussing these problems with me?

These are two obvious ways that client weight issues may surface in therapy: as they seek a comfortable chair or exhibit problems with exertion. However, if we wait for this kind of occurrence to assess how clients feel about their bodies, we could wait an awfully long time. Instead, we need to look for concerns about eating and weight issues everywhere. I do not mean that we should zero in specifically on these problems and ignore all others or that we should turn every session into a discussion about food, but we need to be curious and keep an open mind. Seasoned practitioners are always listening for issues relating to trauma, self-esteem, addiction, and intimacy. Tuning into eating and weight problems requires the same kind of interest, awareness, pattern identification, and active listening.

One area in which eating and weight concerns often surface is self-care. As I have said, just because a client is scrawny or plump does not necessarily mean she has low self-esteem and does not know how to care for herself. However, clients with self-care issues often do neglect or abuse their bodies. Some "forget" to eat, while others are so disconnected from their corporeal self that they overfeed themselves or fail to realize the importance of adequate nutrition. Clients who harbor a great deal of self-hatred often take it out on their bodies, intentionally abusing it by not feeding it when it is hungry and denying it pleasure.

If clients are depressed, they may let themselves go—either by eating too little or too much. They may lack energy to nourish themselves or eat for comfort. They also might not feel good enough about themselves to provide their body with what it needs. Clients may believe they do not deserve to look and feel healthy and fit or view feeding physical needs as a way of saying they can take care of themselves when they do not believe they can.

Ironically, clients who fuss too much over appearance, including obsessing about their weight, may be responding to neglect or abuse from childhood and spend their adulthood trying to make up for it. At heart, they may believe they are worthless or be uncertain and insecure about their value, leading them to develop a polished exterior to compensate for internal inferiority feelings. Over-the-top self-care—that is, needing to look perfect at all times—may hint at body image problems that may, in turn, lead to underlying eating or weight issues.

In fact, many clients who have distorted body image have concerns about food or weight. Some overweight clients do not see their heft; in their mind's eye, they are still the svelte prom queen or athletic jock they were decades before. Society's standards for weight and body mass aside, when a client is not in sync with being oversized, this may indicate disconnection from the body or garden variety denial. Similarly, when a client insists he is fine when he is grossly underweight, there is a distortion in the mind that is serving a purpose. How a client takes a compliment is often telling. She might say that people praise her for being slim, but believe they are lying or trying to make her feel good. At bottom, the problem may be that she never feels thin (or good) enough and is chronically dieting to finally "get there."

Clients who have difficulty regulating affect may turn to or away from food to self-soothe and diminish distress. This does not mean that every client who is labile or poor at handling emotions has eating issues, but that difficulty managing feelings might lead to acting out in the food arena. In fact, clients may not even recognize this behavior as acting out. It may be the only way they know to make themselves feel better and they may view it as acceptable and legitimate, especially if they were brought up to believe that food is the primary way to find comfort or soothe rough edges.

Many clients who have suffered sexual abuse or trauma have eating problems. Discussion about the abuse or trauma should include exploration of past and current ways of coping. Many of these clients used food to comfort themselves and have continued this dysfunctional habit into adulthood. Others turned to food abuse at the time, currently eat "normally," but remain uncomfortable with their body or weight. They may be of average weight but dress provocatively or to conceal sexuality. They may fear gaining weight and diminished sexual attractiveness because beauty or sensuality is the primary way they feel good about themselves. Or they may fear losing weight because they will look more sensual and sexual.

To help the client uncover and express fears of discussing eating and weight issues, ask:

1. Do you ever minimize, deny, or rationalize food and body problems?
2. Do you see your body as others do?
3. Are there any traumatic events in your history that might cause you to feel uncomfortable about your body?
4. How do you take care of yourself physically, emotionally, mentally, and spiritually?

Another area in which food and weight issues arise is intimate and sexual relationships. Clients may become anxious about looking so attractive that they will be hit on, fearing that, given half a chance, they will become highly sexual. Putting on weight may also be a way to distance themselves from their partner, to reject them, or to get back at them for real or imagined slights. Clients may end up putting on weight to prevent them from acting on a desire to end a relationship—if they are fat, who will want them except their partner? Weight gain becomes a way of maintaining the status quo.

When couples are having difficulties, one may get back at the other by either criticizing their partner's weight or eating habits or by undermining her efforts to get to or maintain a healthy weight. It is helpful to listen for these kinds of comments, even when clients say they are in a wonderful, satisfying relationship. Shaming someone about eating and weight is a form of verbal/emotional abuse and is meant to control a partner. In turn, this partner may be acting out with food passive-aggressively. Overweight or even average weight clients also may be preoccupied with slimness if their partner loses a great deal of weight. They may fear that he will abandon them for someone else or be interested in seeing who is available in the dating world. They may go on a crash diet to lose weight to hold on to a partner's affections or be so angry or frightened that they let themselves go so that they will have something on which to blame their anticipated abandonment.

When working with adolescents and young adults who are about to separate from or have recently moved out of a parent's home, it is useful to wonder about the possibility of eating problems. I say eating problems rather than a full-blown disorder because it is common in times of transition for people to eat a little more or less than usual. Maybe young adults are going off to college or for a year abroad or perhaps they are getting their first apartment on their own. Sometimes situational depression, sadness, and longing for home cause loss of appetite. Other times food, especially what Mom or Dad used to make, becomes the best comfort in the world. If a client is buying food for herself for the first time, she may feel a need to break out and try new delights, especially if parental rules about eating were strict. On the other hand, she may purposely restrict food intake in reaction to a family that overfed her and made her eat everything on her plate. Or her parents may have been in charge of feeding her and she may not know how to shop or cook for herself.

Food issues often crop up when clients have a shift in living situation and end up eating with other people. Perhaps a client goes from living alone to having a roommate or to moving in with a few friends. Not only might new foods tempt him, but more socializing might be done around mealtimes that are sit-down dinners rather than grab-what-you-can meals. Maybe he used to go out to dinner with friends once a month and is now in a situation in which, more often than not, meals are a group affair. The reverse situation may also be true, if a client was used to living with another person or a few people and now finds herself living alone. When other people were around, it was easy to count on them for socializing and something to do. Living alone means reaching out to other people and putting effort into finding interesting, meaningful activities. Sometimes food simply is too available and accessible, and it is easier to eat than pick up the phone or go out alone.

Shopping and cooking for other people and being in charge of feeding them can also cause eating problems to flare up. This is especially true for the head of household who was used to winging it with takeout shared with a spouse or partner and who now must consider feeding a family. She might have tried to keep only "healthy" foods in the house before kids came on the scene and now find herself surrounded by foods she previously ate only in restaurants or at parties, including sweets and treats. With children, she will need a wide variety of foods on hand and might be tempted to eat them if she had been restricting them previously. Moreover, working around a family's eating schedule, she may be starving before dinnertime and too exhausted to eat when she is really hungry.

Clients who are homebound due to infirmity, age, or other circumstance may have difficulty regulating their food intake. If they had previously lived a life in which they were frequently out and about, they might be bored staying in and end up eating for excitement. They also may not have much control over grocery shopping and end up eating things they would not ordinarily buy for themselves. Stuck at home with infrequent visitors or occasions to go out, they may give up on self-care and consciously or unconsciously decide to let themselves go and eat whatever they want, whether it is healthy or not. Sometimes, they will eat what is most affordable and accessible, which is often unhealthy processed food, high in salt, sugar, and fat.

Illness and medication may also cause changes in eating and/or weight. Some diseases, including celiac disease, Crohn's disease, certain cancers, malnutrition, ulcers, dementia, HIV, tumors, chronic intestinal problems, and hyperthyroidism lead to weight loss. Other conditions may produce weight gain, including hypothyroidism, deficiency in essential fatty acids, food sensitivities, Cushing's syndrome, blood/sugar imbalance, and kidney, heart, or liver disease. Medications such as steroids, antihistamines, hormone replacement therapy, oral contraceptives, cortisone, beta-blockers, many classes of antidepressants, lithium, antipsychotics, anti-convulsants, antihypertensives, alpha-blockers, and migraine, heartburn, diabetes, and breast cancer drugs may also cause weight gain. Heartburn and anti-seizure medications may also cause weight gain in some and weight loss in others.

Clients going through any kind of emotional upheaval or life transition may have unexpected, involuntary shifts in eating patterns and fluctuations in weight. It may take time for a client to adjust to a different eating schedule after starting a new job. A client planning a wedding may be too excited to eat or so anxious that all she does is pick at food. A recent widower may lose his appetite, as may one who has lost a job or home, or is forced into a situation against his will. In crisis, a client who has been an overeater may suffer loss of appetite, while another who always has been in control of her eating may let loose and be unable to resist temptation. Whenever a client is suddenly side-lined from exercise for a long period of time due to injury, illness, or other circumstance, he may find himself eating more or gaining weight on the same amount of food he has always eaten.

Cultural expectations may promote changes in weight or eating. If a client is new to this country, he may want to conform to American expectations of how he should eat and look. He may not even realize that he feels pressured to gain or lose weight. His eating might change as he expands his food horizons and tries to fit in. Moreover, the sheer stress of living in an unfamiliar culture might affect his appetite. Cultural pressures may also play a part if someone marries into another ethnic group in which appreciation of food or a certain body type is valued. A client trying to be accepted into an Italian family that loves to feast may find herself putting on weight just to please her in-laws. An overweight client with a partner whose family is Japanese or Chinese might feel ashamed of his size and feel pressure to slim down.

Clients who have recently given up an addiction—smoking, drinking, taking illegal or prescription drugs, shopping, sex, or gambling, for example—may be vulnerable to switching vices and turn to food. A client who stops smoking will find that food tastes better now that he is not deadening his taste buds, and he may use food to meet oral cravings. A client who has previously spent a good deal of time going out and drinking, drugging, gambling, or shopping might look for a quick rush in food or feel stuck at home—safe from her addiction—with nothing to do but eat. Interestingly, sometimes weight gain may be positive for a client in recovery from drug addiction or alcoholism because it may mean he is taking better care of himself nutritionally.

If a client is severely depressed, she may turn to or away from food. On the one hand, she may eat, especially carbohydrates, to try to feel better. On the other hand, she may lose her appetite and taste for foods she has traditionally enjoyed and have no interest in feeding herself. Additionally, clients who are depressed often have a desire to eat but no energy to shop or cook for themselves, so that they end up shedding pounds or eating junk food that is easily accessible.

To help the client recognize other problems that might be affecting eating and weight, ask:

1. Have you made any major changes in your life recently that may cause a shift in appetite?
2. Have you gone through any recent crisis that may cause a change in appetite?
3. How do the expectations of others play into your eating?
4. Might you have an increased or decreased appetite because you are depressed?
5. Do you have any other addictions or have you recently given up anything you were addicted to?
6. Would more information on nutrition or how to shop or cook improve your relationship with food?

In terms of assessing client weight and eating concerns, there are no rules of thumb or specific approaches that work better than others. During the time that we become acquainted with the client and do our initial assessment, we might or might not mention our observations. Because part of any clinical assessment is learning how open the client is to new ideas and feedback, we must use our judgment about the information we are acquiring regarding the client's attitudes toward and behaviors around eating and weight. Whether we share our observations as we go along or wait until we recognize patterns that need addressing is up to us. Opportunities will be missed and new opportunities will arise. There is no exact moment that is more right than another to share clinical knowledge. Chapter 11, "Treatment Options," will provide clinicians with general approaches and specific avenues for using the information about eating and weight issues gained through assessment.

CHAPTER 7

Clinical
Disorders

Sometimes eating and weight problems stand alone and sometimes they coexist with other disorders—depressive, anxiety,
dissociative, or personality disorders. Obviously there are many people who are anxious and depressed who are "normal" eaters, as well as
dysfunctional eaters who lack underlying mood or character disorders.
The whole subject of who has what can be very confusing to both client
and therapist. The best we can do is to be alert to the fact that food and
weight problems often are related to imbalanced biochemistry and/or
distorted thinking and take it from there.

There are two ways to think about potential links between mood
disorders and food problems. One is to be open to the idea that anyone
who meets, or even partially meets, the criteria for these psychological
classifications may suffer from a disregulation of neurotransmitters
such as serotonin, norepinephrine, GABA, dopamine, and other
assorted chemicals. That means considering that if clients are having
difficulty regulating affect, they *also* may have difficulty regulating
appetite and may be abusing food to modulate feelings. The other
approach is to consider that clients who abuse food might have underlying neurotransmitter imbalances that produce mood disturbance.

In trying to connect the dots between food, weight, body issues, and clinical disorders, remember that each manifests in a unique way within an individual. No two clients will have exactly the same dysfunctional patterns and it is wise to expect the unexpected. One client may drink and overeat when depressed; another may smoke cigarettes to calm agitation or to control weight. A client may become so anxious due to problems at work or home that he rapidly puts on 10 pounds or may be so caught up in running around trying to resolve a crisis that he forgets to eat. I once treated a client who initially lost her appetite after separating and moving out from her husband, only to find that a few weeks later she was lonely and eating everything in sight.

When clients who regularly overeat become depressed or anxious and lose their appetite, they are more often than not overjoyed and may make jokes about being on the "depression diet." They may even end up having mixed feelings about their unhappiness or agitation, disliking it, but loving the result of diminished interest in food. I have known clients who have refused to go on an antidepressant, preferring unhappiness combined with decreased appetite to an improved mood and regaining weight.

Almost any psychological condition can be associated with eating problems. The following disorder classifications may be (but are not necessarily) found in people suffering from eating problems: obsessive compulsive, depressive, post traumatic stress, bipolar and bipolar II, borderline personality, panic, generalized anxiety, attention deficit, dissociative, and multiple personality.

Depressive Disorders

As with eating problems, depression exists on a continuum, from major depressive disorder to bipolar to dysthymia. Although there is evidence that people with eating disorders tend to suffer from other mental health disorders like anxiety or depression, and that low levels of serotonin may exist in people with eating disorders and depression, this is only proof of correlation, not causation. Depression also has been associated with bulimia through a measurable change in neurotransmitter activity and mood before and after eating and purging.

One obvious connection is that eating or weight fluctuation is a criterion for depressive disorders. According to the *DSM-IV-R*, a symptom of major depressive disorder is "significant weight loss when not dieting or weight gain (for example, a change of more than 5% of body weight in a month), or decrease or increase in appetite nearly every day" (APA, 1994, p. 327); diagnostic criteria for dysthymic disorder include "poor appetite or overeating" (p. 349); and one of the symptoms of depression with melancholic features is "significant anorexia or weight loss" (p. 384).

Although a problem with neurotransmitters may be the cause of depression, anxiety, and difficulties with food, we cannot know that from interviewing clients. We may find clients who have had eating and weight issues long before they became depressed or who have suffered from depression since childhood, with onset of food and weight problems occurring in adolescence or adulthood. There are clients whose depression is exacerbated by being overweight, but it may not be clear whether the primary reason they isolate is because they are fat, ashamed, and find it hard to get around, or because they are too lethargic and inert to get up and go. We may run into clients who have been able to restrain a tendency toward overeating for decades who suddenly fall into situational depression which overwhelms them and leads to out-of-control eating.

Clients may suffer from low self-esteem and become depressed over time because they cannot get a handle on their eating problems or lose sufficient weight to feel satisfied with their body. No matter how successful they are in other aspects of life, they may let their size define them and be unable to get past feeling defective and abnormal. Living in this anti-fat, thin-obsessed society, they are constantly treated as if they are not okay as is and need to change, do not take adequate care of themselves, and as if it is their fault that they are fat. We cannot underestimate the impact that a barrage of negative messages—for some overweight people over the span of a lifetime—can have on the ego. It is a short slide from not feeling good about yourself to experiencing yourself as worthless and unsalvageable.

Although some thin clients may have a chipper, upbeat exterior, scratch the surface and you may find that they suffer from underlying depression. In fact, very often the only thing these clients feel good about *is* their slimness. They use dieting to keep up their spirits and motivation to take care of themselves and often become depressed when they give up rigid food regimes. Clients may also get worn down and become depressed from years of bulimia, hoarding food, or secret binge eating. They bear tremendous shame about these behaviors and may feel they deserve to be depressed because of how bad they are.

One of the most obvious signs of depression is loss of appetite, but this does not necessarily signal an eating problem. In fact, when a relatively "normal" eater stops eating because of a low mood, that is a clear sign of depression. Usually, when a client begins taking an antidepressant, appetite returns to its premorbid level. Unless the client continues to bring up eating problems, we can assume that the temporary loss of appetite was depression related.

To assess whether the client's eating problems are related to depression, ask:

1. Are you eating more or less than you do when you are not depressed?
2. How much do food abuse and weight issues affect how depressed you feel?
3. Does your eating feel more under control when you're on antidepressants?

4. (for an overweight client) Are you less depressed when you lose weight?
5. (for an underweight client) Are you less or more depressed when you gain weight?
6. How can I help you handle depression more effectively?

Generalized Anxiety Disorder

Although no eating- or weight-related criteria appear under "Anxiety Disorders" in *DSM-IV-R*, most of us have known clients who eat more or less when they are tense and stressed. In fact, a person need not have eating problems per se to crave carbohydrates when they are wound up. The fact is that anxiety disorders frequently co-occur with eating disorders, likely due to an imbalance of neurotransmitters causing both conditions.

It is not surprising that people who are uptight and high-strung may have difficulty self-soothing. Although many would not think of turning to food when they are a bundle of nerves or restless, others would not think of looking anywhere else for comfort. If a client is inclined to view food as special and magical and as a reward, especially if her parents used food to round off their rough edges, it is likely that food will become her primary support as well. On the other hand, anxious clients also bind emotions by obsessing about things like recipes, weight, and what to wear that will make them look thin. Whereas one anxious, overweight client might become deeply depressed thinking about how to dress for an upcoming reunion, another might detour her nervousness into going on a crash diet to slim down.

Anxiety and fear are major components of eating problems: a client's terror of gaining 2 pounds because 2 will turn into 6, which will morph into 20; fear of being ridiculed and excluded for being fat, based on past experience or on unfounded anticipation; anxiety that the food police will come rushing in if food is left unfinished or if leftovers are thrown away; fears of being hungry and deprived, both real and imagined; and nervousness about eating enough to please others or so much that they will get upset or angry.

Clients who are anxious might not even connect their eating to their inner turmoil. They may not realize that they are ruminating or running upcoming scenarios over and over in their mind. Many anxious clients are unaware that overeating or eating when they are not hungry is due to a heightened affectual state because they are disconnected from their emotions. They may call themselves hyper, highstrung, or driven, and not recognize that they are in a constant state of arousal and vigilance. They may only know that they feel better after they eat (especially carbohydrates), but not make a connection between agita and increased appetite.

To assess the client's anxiety and eating problems, ask:

1. Do you eat more or less when you are anxious?
2. How do you know when you are anxious?
3. How does food help when you are anxious?
4. If you don't eat when you are anxious, what do you think will happen?
5. How can I help you handle anxiety more effectively?

Obsessive-Compulsive Disorder (OCD)

Eating problems that are ongoing and become the center of a client's life have much in common with OCD. For the record, *obsessions* are "recurrent and persistent thoughts, impulses, or images that are experienced . . . as intrusive and inappropriate and that cause marked anxiety or distress. *Compulsions* are "repetitive behaviors . . . or mental acts . . . that a client feels driven to perform in response to an obsession, or according to the rules that must be applied rigidly" (APA, 1994, p. 418).

Many clients will say right off that they are obsessed with food or with being or getting thin. Although it is unlikely that they have the specific criteria of OCD in mind, they know an obsession when they feel one. They will tell you that they think about food 24/7, that being thin or losing weight crowds out thoughts of family or work, that they cannot control their thinking though they have tried with all their heart and soul. If they could, they would rip open their heads and yank out their thoughts to get relief.

Some clients recognize that the problem is in their minds and some do not (those with body dysmorphic disorder, in particular). They know on some level that having intense distress and a preoccupation with food and their body is abnormal and unhealthy. If they obsess about weight, they recognize that their desire to be thin or thinner is more about chasing an elusive ideal of perfection than pursuing a realistic dream. If they obsess about food, they understand that it is not nutrients they crave but emotional gratification or oblivion. Nevertheless, knowing that their thinking is irrational does not stop it and they may struggle on and off all day long with intrusive thoughts about weighing themselves or food calling to them. These thoughts can be so intrusive that they make life, in general, exceedingly problematic, depending on the runaway nature of their thoughts and their ability to control them.

Clients describe their actions as compulsive (hence, the term *compulsive eating*). They talk about "going unconscious," or being in a fugue- or foglike state—coming to as they scrape the bottom of the Häagen-Dazs container or are tossing away the empty bag of Cheez

Doodles. They tell you that they went into the bathroom to grab some aspirin and could not resist hopping on the scale, though they had weighed themselves not an hour before. Often clients believe and feel that they are totally powerless in the face of inner forces that drive them to food behaviors they abhor. Clients who must eat at a certain time, weigh their food to the nth of an ounce, need to maintain a particular order of food intake, or engage in a ritual that goes along with eating certain or all foods are in the grip of compulsions. And then there are those who, once they start to eat, have to finish everything— the whole box, bag, jar, or the entire meal. There is no in between, no flexibility in regulating appetite; behavior is all or nothing.

A client might panic because a guest ate something in his refrigerator that he had planned to eat himself. Some clients will only go out to eat at a specific hour, no earlier or later. Others have to know the caloric and fat content of every morsel that goes into their mouth or will count out 9 crackers but never 10, five carrot sticks but never six, to eat every day, day after day. Although these behaviors may seem amusing, they are anything but.

The goal of this behavior is not really about food, but to prevent anticipated, or lessen current, anxiety. The most helpful paradigm of obsessive-compulsive disorder (OCD) is educating clients about how obsessive thinking is reinforced by compulsive actions and vice versa, so that they can understand that they will have to tolerate some discomfort—in this case, anxiety—in order to reduce or eliminate unhealthy eating patterns.

To assess the client's food abuse as obsession and compulsion, ask:

1. How often do you have intrusive thoughts about eating, calorie counting, weighing yourself, or anything else related to food?

2. What do you think will happen if you don't follow
   through on compulsions that drive you to obsessive food
   behavior?
3. Do you have other obsessions and compulsions?
4. How can I help you manage your food obsessions and
   compulsions more effectively?

Sexual Trauma and Dissociative Disorders

More and more studies are being done on the correlation between
sexual trauma—such as molestation, rape, and incest—and eating
disorders. The following summary echoes research in the field:
"Young girls who are sexually abused are more likely to develop eating disorders as adolescents . . . and findings add to a growing body of
research suggesting that trauma in childhood increases the risk of an
eating disorder. Abused girls were more dissatisfied with their weight
and more likely to diet and purge. . . . Abused girls were also more
likely to restrict their eating when they were bored or emotionally
upset, and [. . .] abused girls might experience higher levels of emotional distress, possibly linked to their abuse, and have trouble coping" (Wonderlich, Crosby, Mitchell, Roberts, Haseltine, Demuth, &
Thompson, 2000, p. 1283).

Kearney-Cooke and Ackard (1999) evaluated the differences
between females who had been sexually abused and those who had not
on aspects such as body image, self-image, self-consciousness, and relationships with others. They found that females who had been sexually
abused reported more body dissatisfaction, more self-consciousness,
and less satisfaction with themselves in their relationships. Some of the
detrimental effects of sexual abuse included dissatisfaction with and
lack of control over the body, low self-esteem, increased self-

consciousness, and poor sex life and relations with men. Women who had been abused also were more likely to have eating disorders.

It is not surprising that a client who has been sexually violated may have body and food regulation issues due to feelings of powerlessness, breaking of trust, unworthiness, and fear of intimacy. Although the majority of studies are being done with females, it is prudent to consider that a male client who has been sexually abused may also have eating and body image problems. Depending on other factors—difficulties with impulse control, affect regulation, substance abuse, poor self-care, and major intimacy issues—it is not unreasonable to wonder if (though certainly not to assume that) a client with eating, weight, and body-image problems may have had some kind of sexual trauma.

For most of us, the clients we counsel with dissociative disorders are few and far between. Although we may see some who misremember the past or have only a foggy notion of what it was like, most individuals on our caseload do not have fugue states or multiple personalities. However, it makes sense that clients who have been traumatized enough to dissociate may have problems staying connected to reality and to their body.

Dissociation is defined as "a disruption in the usually integrated functions of consciousness, memory, identity, or perception of the environment. The disturbance may be sudden or gradual, transient or chronic" (APA, 1994, p. 766). A milder form of loss of conscious functioning is described by Geneen Roth, author of many books on eating, as "going unconscious." Clients do not fall into a true trance, but often describe the state of eating until they are sick or exhausted as dreamlike. They insist they do not remember what led them to eating, but suddenly found themselves with an empty box of cereal and a full belly; they recall little about throwing on a coat in the dead of night and driving to the 7-Eleven for a bagful of snacks, only to awaken the next morning to a floor strewn with cookie and candy wrappers.

My point is not to pathologize clients who lose touch with reality when they are in the throes of food abuse, but to make clear how debil-itating and frightening loss of control is, how on the edge of deeper, more serious dysfunction. With clients who have such a profound dis-connect from their minds and bodies, we need to tread lightly and carefully. They generally have good reason for going unconscious at specific moments. Perhaps they were not sexually or physically abused, but might have endured horrific fights between their parents in which their only solace was sneaking down to the kitchen and up to their room to eat in silence and safety. They may not be reacting to something terrible that was actively done to them, but to being raised in an environment in which staying conscious all the time was simply too scary and painful.

To assess if the client has suffered sexual trauma and may dissociate relating to food, ask:

1. Do you have reason to believe you have suffered sexual trauma or been abused?
2. Do you generally feel connected or disconnected from your body? How about when you're eating?
3. Do you ever feel as if you're looking at yourself eating while consuming food (that is, are you both the eater and onlooker)?
4. Do you ever find you've eaten but were not aware of doing so at the time or don't remember eating?
5. What do you generally remember right before your unconscious eating experience and right after?

In many cases, we are already treating a client for depression or anxiety when we discover she has an eating problem. Other times, it becomes obvious that some underlying condition is driving her difficulties with food and we refocus on what they may be. The goal is to make no assumptions and ensure that we leave no stone unturned when trying to discover the origins of food and weight problems. There is no one avenue to help clients with dual diagnosis of food and other conditions, but Chapter 11, "Treatment Options," will provide alternative approaches. As always, the best therapeutic route will come from keen observation and an open mind.

CHAPTER 8

Life-Cycle
Issues

S ome of our clients might have had the stage set for them to have eating problems even before they were born. They may not have received adequate nourishment as a growing fetus and were low-birth-weight babies who suffered from malnutrition at birth. Maybe as infants they were colicky eaters or fussy nursers, had childhood medical conditions or illnesses that affected their ability to take in food, or received insufficient or inappropriate nutrition due to poverty or neglect. Other clients may have sailed through their first decade eating normally and being of average weight, but developed problems in adolescence as a reaction to raging hormones, family problems, or peer or social pressures.

On the other hand, clients may have been comfortable around food and in their bodies for most of their lives and suddenly, due to physiological shifts, psychological changes, or external circumstance (or a combination), found themselves eating or weighing more or less. Additionally, people who never worried about their weight simply might find that the number on the scale starts to creep up as they age and become less active. Although we might think of eating disorders as occurring mostly in adolescence and young adulthood—and the numbers would prove us right for anorexia and bulimia—people encounter food problems at any age or stage of life.

Childhood

That said, there are certain times, what we call critical periods, when vulnerability to eating issues increases. Due to hormonal changes and the often tough transition from childhood to adulthood, we used to see clients come to therapy with food problems around the time of or shortly after puberty. It was not unusual to hear from high schoolers, and occasionally those in junior high, that they felt uncomfortable in their bodies and wanted to be thinner or that they were feeling family pressure to slim down.

In the past, children were occasionally sent to therapy for being overweight when all else failed: diets, doctors, behavioral plans, exercise, and nutritionists. Their parents wanted them to drop some weight and hoped that talk therapy, especially with a behavioral bent, might motivate them or keep them on track. In other cases, obese children were sent to therapy to learn to feel better about themselves and to develop effective ways to handle the bullying and teasing that often comes from being larger than schoolmates and friends. Our job was to help these children with the results of weight excess as well as to support them in shedding pounds.

These days, however, children are fatter than ever—10% of toddlers between ages 2 and 5 are seriously overweight, 15% of children 6 through 19 are overweight, and 13% of children 6 through 19 are obese, a number that has tripled in the last 2 decades—and therapy has become adjunctive to diets, medication, nutritionists, and exercise plans to help young clients take and keep weight off ("General Eating Disorder Fact Sheet," MEDA Web Site).

In addition to treating more and more overweight youth, we are seeing escalating numbers of children of normal weight who are preoccupied with thinness. Sometimes they are fine with their growing bodies, but their parents believe they are too chubby. Let's remember that by the time they have reached fourth grade, more children have been on a diet than not! Other studies tell us that children as young as 6 are expressing body dissatisfaction and weight concerns, that 42% of girls in the first through third grades want to be thinner, and that 51% of 9- and 10-year-old girls say they feel better about themselves when they are on a diet ("General Eating Disorder Fact Sheet," MEDA Web site). These statistics are shocking and do not even touch on the escalating number of teens obsessed with getting skinny and addicted to diets, something we have come to expect in the last 2 or 3 decades.

Because of their innocence and ignorance, children who end up in therapy due to eating and weight issues cannot possibly imagine how disordered eating might affect them physically in terms of body growth, nutrition, and future health problems. Even the child who has an anorexic, openly bulimic, or binge eating parent cannot fully understand how a failure to meet specific developmental milestones will inhibit their ability to develop and mature physically, interpersonally, and emotionally.

Nor do most of them realize that it is natural for children to have body fat because they are still growing. Inundated with pictures of teen celebrities who are virtually fat-free, children start to believe that no one—no matter what their age—should have any meat on their bones. Unfortunately, many of their parents reinforce this falsehood and too many latency-age children are encouraged by their parents to focus on body weight and appearance when they should be thinking about health and fitness.

The focus of childhood eating problems falls into two categories. The first is when children are overweight or obese and have low self-esteem. Because of their size, it is not uncommon for them to be bullied, teased, or excluded from neighborhood or school activities. In these cases, therapy can teach them how to stand up for themselves or ignore others' insults. Care must be given to building self-esteem, which means helping them feel good about their unique abilities and talents, encouraging them to develop positive relationships with other children, and guiding them toward finding success in school, with their family, and within the community.

Whenever possible, parents should be brought in to assess the family situation to find out if the child is also being bullied/taunted/shamed at home, to explore parental response to what is going on outside the family, and to make parents part of an effective treatment plan. Because being persecuted and teased is one the worst things that can happen to a child, very often school personnel must be informed of the situation, including making plans to deal with harassers, teaching children how to relate to each other more acceptably, and instituting a zero-tolerance policy regarding specific unacceptable behaviors.

Assessment also includes understanding how family dynamics may contribute to a child's eating problems, whether she is hoarding food or eating it in secret, and what parental attitudes are about eating and weight. Sometimes a child eats to tune out parental bickering. Often the child is overfed because, to the feeder, food equals love, or because in the family culture food and eating are highly important. If parents do not have healthy eating habits, they may need a referral to a dietician or nutritionist who can educate them about hunger, cravings, food choice and enjoyment, and how to help themselves and their children stop eating when they have had enough. They may also need information about the importance of exercise, nutrition, and fitness.

The second category of children who wind up in our office due to a food disturbance is those who enter treatment because they are dieting or starving themselves. Once again, the therapist will want to involve the family. Although occasionally a child might succumb to cutting calories due to social pressure, it is more than likely that the young girl (and it is usually a female) is getting subtle or covert messages at home about thinness and fatness or that a low sense of self-worth inclines the child to overvalue thinness. Meeting with parents and other family members (including siblings or older relatives who live in the household) is essential to assessing what their eating and weight issues are, understanding how they might affect the child's food intake and body image, and correcting unhealthy messages and dysfunctional relationships.

Family difficulties that may lead to a child developing disordered eating and an obsession with thinness include: a child being embarrassed or teased about Mom or Dad being obese; one or both parents habitually expressing anti-fat sentiments and extolling slimness; parents who pressure a child to be perfect; ongoing battles over food and weight; other family members who inappropriately try to control a child's eating or weight; or parents who struggle with their own food intake and the scale (most often through chronic dieting) in such a way that they model poor eating behaviors and preoccupation with fatness and thinness. Occasionally it is live-in grandparents or extended family members who express dissatisfaction with a child's weight, with or without parents' knowledge. Obviously, food and body problems in a young child may also be indicative of sexual abuse, and we should be alert to that possibility.

Most children are openly and anxiously looking for answers and their problems can often be resolved by education and straightening out family dynamics. These young clients also need encouragement to develop different aspects of themselves and become well-rounded (no pun intended) so that they do not base feeling good about themselves solely on appearance. Success may involve getting a child more or less involved in activities and helping her choose friends who are not preoccupied with looks and popularity to the exclusion of self-development.

Because children often cannot distinguish healthy from unhealthy behavior, it is important to gently inquire about a child's eating habits and body image. A child might not realize that there is anything wrong with taking food into his room to eat in private when his parents are fighting downstairs, or that regularly skipping breakfast and throwing away lunch to lose weight will harm her growing body. Even if children know that specific behaviors are not good for them, they may be filled with shame and not mention them because they are afraid of being seen as bad. In fact, whenever there is mild to serious family dysfunction, it is a good idea to check in with a child about food and body problems, even if the child does not raise them.

Reflections for Therapist

1. Is there any indication that a (child) client might have eating or weight problems? What are these indications? What do you need to ask to find out?
2. How might what you know about the family or its dynamics reinforce these problems? How might what you know help to alleviate them?
3. Are there community resources to help educate the parents about "normal" and healthy eating?
4. If the child is being teased or bullied because of his weight, how can you get the school involved in stopping this behavior?
5. If the child is obsessed with dieting, how will you help him understand how dangerous dieting can be?
6. Could sexual abuse be causing eating or body problems?

Adolescence

Adolescence has always been a time of turbulence and turmoil, a period of bodily changes and intense roller-coaster emotions, of shifting alliances from family to peers, and of self-discovery by trial and error. It is understandable that adolescents may want to experiment with eating more or less (dieting or binge eating) as they observe what friends do and see the examples set by celebrities and other adults. What is saddening is not that teens seek out dieting as a way to rein in shifting appetites and raging hormones, but the intensity of body hate that drives starvation and the relentlessness of their adolescent pursuit of thinness and abhorrence of fat.

Current estimates are that 63% of high school girls and 16.2% of boys are on a diet at any given time and, although we know that not everyone who diets will develop an eating disorder, chronic dieting is considered the gateway behavior into eating dysfunction and body image problems. More than 1 in 10 girls in grades 9 through 12 and almost 1 in 20 same-age boys have at least five symptoms of bulimia ("General Eating Disorder Fact Sheet," MEDA Web site). One-half to 1% of adolescents have anorexia nervosa and 2–3% of adolescents have bulimia nervosa ("Statistics and Study Findings," Eating Disorders Coalition Web site). These numbers are growing, as eating disorders develop at earlier ages and become more severe and prevalent.

Dealing with adolescents who have eating and weight issues can be highly challenging because their habits have become more ingrained than young children's, they may be more secretive, peer pressure is stronger, hormones have a greater impact on their biology, and they may very well want to engage in struggle with authority figures. Nevertheless, progress can be made by making a strong alliance with the client (and her family), being supportive, improving self-esteem, providing education, strengthening healthy family dynamics, and being aware of and sidestepping power struggles.

Adolescents may believe that dieting is the norm and the right thing to do and that people must be thin to be happy, popular, and successful. Most teenagers have no idea how dangerous eating disorders can be by setting the stage for more serious problems later in life or that they can actually reach a point of no return and die from them. Or, more accurately, they may know this information intellectually, but believe that it will never happen to them.

For some teen clients, providing statistics on how diets may lead to eating disorders helps them put the issue into perspective, but warnings alone are not generally productive. Moreover, lecturing an adolescent about food, weight, or exercise is not only the death knell for cognitive or behavioral change, but will likely increase acting out. Generally beneficial therapeutic tactics include serious discussions about celebrities with eating disorders, establishing life goals, education about emotional and physical health, affect management, and teaching clients how to think for themselves and buck the crowd.

It is useful to explore what is going on for the adolescent who keeps herself focused on food and weight in order to expose and correct irrational thinking. Tip-offs that clients might be overly concerned with weight include intense desire to fit in with a particular peer group, yearning for popularity, insisting on getting to or maintaining an ultra-low weight for sports competition, and a preoccupation with appearance. Once again, family therapy is extremely useful in assessing and altering family dynamics that may impinge on a teenager transitioning into adulthood effectively—without eating and body-image problems. Even when parents refuse therapy, a systems model is almost always the one to use with teens in individual therapy to get the family into healthy equilibrium.

To help the child or adolescent client understand her eating and weight problems, ask:

1. How is your eating? Do you enjoy food? What are mealtimes like at your house?
2. How do you feel about your body? Do you think you're fat, thin, or just right?

3. How important are appearance, fitting in, and popularity? How important are they to your parents?

4. What pressure do you get from peers to be thin and popular?

5. Are you engaged in any sports competitions that require you to keep a low weight?

6. What do your parents, relatives, and friends say about your eating or weight?

7. Do you ever steal food, hide it, or eat it in secret?

8. Do you ever not eat because you are afraid of getting fat? Do you ever binge eat?

College and Young Adulthood

Some teens who begin having eating problems in junior high or high school (or earlier) continue to have them postgraduation. Alternately, some adolescents have a comfortable relationship with food and their bodies until they head off to college (whether they live at home or move close by or far away) or take their first adult job. Those in late adolescence often do not feel self-sufficient or comfortable with autonomy in spite of the fact that they are considered and treated as adults, and may play out their inner struggles with extreme changes in eating.

Much has been written about eating dysfunction as a symptom of separation and individuation problems at this transitional time, and most of it is true. An eating problem is a way for a young adult to still get lots of parental concern and attention, and may indicate difficulty in the family letting the child go. An eating problem can symbolize or point toward trouble with self-care and using sound judgment as well as deeply mixed attitudes about competence, self-trust, and self-confidence. In these situations, the client usually transfers feelings about the parent onto the therapist and plays out her struggles over autonomy in the therapy. The therapist may need to do a great deal of interpreting of behavior—identifying and fishing for feelings that generate it—and must focus on helping the client resolve her internal conflicts about growing up and being on her own.

Statistics about eating disorders, especially females during late adolescence, are scary and disheartening. More than 91% of those with eating disorders are adolescent and young adult women. 91% of female college students surveyed had attempted to control their weight through dieting and 22% said they dieted "often" or "always." Almost one fifth of college-aged women in the United States are bulimic. Most female sufferers of anorexia are between the ages of 12 and 25 ("Statistics," National Eating Disorders Association Web site).

Changes in eating in young adulthood need not be pathological, but may be a way of testing limits. The client who was overfed by parents and never left the table without being stuffed may be in charge of feeding herself for the first time and may cut way back on food and go a little too far. The client who is no longer deprived of food or restricted from eating by his parents might go a bit overboard, eating all the foods he was forbidden from eating and rapidly putting on weight. Clients may become frightened of these unexpected reactions to food and benefit from guidance on how to be proactive with eating and weight rather than reactive to previous family experiences.

Young adulthood is also a time when clients encounter new life stresses and may avoid distressing emotions by becoming preoccupied with thinness and dieting or by overeating and binge eating. Too often clients have depended on their parents to help modulate their internal turmoil (and, too frequently, parents are willing to play this role beyond a time when it is age-appropriate) and have minimal ability to self-soothe or regulate feelings. Because food is accessible and food abuse (under- or overeating) is a peer-acceptable solution to affective discomfort, it makes sense that they would turn to it rather than develop improved coping skills. In this case, the therapist's work is to help clients enlarge their capacity for emotional management and make sure they have supportive, healthy networks of friends and family from whom they can get comfort and feedback when necessary.

To help young adult clients understand that new stresses might lead to disordered eating and preoccupation with weight, ask:

1. How are you handling the new stresses in your life? Do you regularly manage uncomfortable feelings by eating or not eating or by obsessing about weight?
2. How do you feel about being on your own?
3. What is it like making decisions and living with the consequences? Is it harder or easier than you expected?
4. What were your eating and weight like in childhood and adolescence?
5. What are you most concerned with regarding food and weight?
6. Would you like help learning new coping skills in this stressful time of your life? How else might I help you?

Dating and Mating

Although not every client who is seeking a date or a mate becomes focused or overfocused on how much they weigh, many do, especially women. Both males and females who have previously been content with their weight may enter their early or late 20s and suddenly think about slimming down and toning up. Others who have yo-yoed up and down on the scale may finally decide to get serious about eating healthily and begin to exercise regularly. Still others who have been overweight may be motivated to shed pounds to feel more attractive and make themselves more eligible in the dating market.

Because being thin is so (overly) valued in this society, it is not uncommon for underweight women to redouble their efforts to stay slim when they hit the dating scene, for two reasons. The first is that dating can be stressful and dieting and preoccupation with food may be such an ingrained pattern for managing stress that this obsession may increase. The second is that many women are brainwashed to believe that "no one (meaning no female) can ever be too rich or too thin." Far too many women are convinced that slenderness is the ticket to popularity and equate becoming thinner with having more dates.

Sometimes clients who have been minimizing overeating or weight problems finally decide to face them squarely when they become interested in dating in general or in striking up or deepening a relationship with one person in particular. Because our job is to assist clients in both establishing and reaching their goals, this is a golden opportunity to help them examine their dysfunctional eating habits. However, we need to be careful and not encourage them to buy into the thin-is-better myth. Exploring eating and weight issues through the lens of improved health and fitness is a far more productive approach.

We must be careful with clients of average weight not to get seduced into their thinking that they must lose weight to find romance. We need to encourage them to examine why they believe that losing weight will help in the dating department, especially through discussing experiences that have caused them to think this way. Moreover, we must make sure that they do not become one-sided in their quest for self-improvement, that is, putting more energy into enhancing their appearance by losing weight than in developing qualities that would make them a healthier, more well-rounded individual.

Although there is some pressure on men to be slim to be attractive, it is not nearly the burden it is for women. Research tells us that males are more likely to want to take off weight to be healthy and fit. However, depending on their history and no matter what they now weigh, men who have been overweight during childhood or adolescence may still carry around painful memories of being teased or rejected because they were fat. Talking about these experiences in therapy helps remove the sting, but we cannot expect that men who have had difficulty with intimate relationships in the past will suddenly feel confident. Much work will need to be done on their beliefs and expectations about being judged, on self-esteem, and on the potential to self-sabotage relationships due to fear of rejection and abandonment.

Some clients who were overweight earlier in life lose weight but retain their insecurity about dating. They may find that it was easier when they were fat because they had something on which to blame rejection. Now they feel more vulnerable and sensitive to an unreturned phone call or someone turning them down for a date. These clients need help understanding that everyone gets rejected romantically at one time or another—whether fat, thin, or in between—and that they should not personalize a "no" response. Others who were previously overweight may equate being thin with being sexual and popular and try to make up for lost adolescent or early adulthood time by having a great many sexual partners. Generally they feel an immediate rush at being desired, which is followed by an inner emptiness when good feelings gradually dissipate. Our job is to help them see that there is more to being popular than appearance.

Another circumstance in which eating and weight may become an issue is when partners marry or begin living together. Clients who have carefully monitored their weight and controlled it by having only limited foods around are now subject to more variety and temptation. Moreover, those who have become or stayed thin in order to find a mate may relax their habits once they start sharing space and affection. Add to that the stress that commitment to a relationship and living in close quarters generates, and eating may be an area in which disturbances start to show up.

New foods, going grocery shopping together, a shift in eating schedules, and shared mealtimes might all trigger changes in eating habits. Spouses who went from their parents' home right into marriage might be used to the big meals their mothers made, while long-single newlyweds might be accustomed to getting takeout most nights and eating leftovers the rest of the week. Some might want to eat only low-calorie, low-fat foods and refuse to let their partners bring goodies and treats into the house. Others might be unwilling to forgo having a variety of delicious foods around, making it enormously difficult for eating disordered partners not to end up binge eating. Combining appetites can be like integrating families, and a bigger deal than anyone expects.

To help the client assess eating and weight concerns regarding dating and mating, ask:

1. How concerned are you about your weight in terms of dating and finding a mate?
2. Does your focus on food change when you contemplate dating? When you are on a date? When you are in a relationship?
3. What is the biggest problem for you regarding food and relationships?
4. Where are the pressures about eating and weight coming from in your life—family, friends, dates, a partner, yourself?
5. How can I help you feel better about dating, intimacy, and commitment?

— —

Getting Pregnant and Pregnancy

For women who have had lifelong food problems, the desire to get pregnant and have a child is often the motivation needed to make changes in their eating habits and how they view their body. Instead of striving to improve their appearance, they may, instead, start focusing on how to become healthier and more fit. Undereaters may allow themselves to gain weight because they desire to be healthy enough to get pregnant, and overeaters may decide to eat more nutritiously and cut calories, anticipating the extra pounds of pregnancy.

Of course, the opposite effect also may hold true: Overweight clients might allow themselves to eat more because they are "eating for two," while those who strive for thinness may cut calories in fear of anticipated pregnancy-related weight gain. Some women throw themselves into healthy eating so intensely during pregnancy that they end up feeling deprived of foods they love and end up bingeing on them. Whatever the case, our work is to help clients see that what they are doing in the eating arena must support a healthful pregnancy and a healthy baby.

For women who have had long-standing weight and eating problems, pregnancy may exacerbate or alleviate concerns. They may feel relief that, for the first time in their lives, they no longer have to worry about looking svelte and can be fat without caring. Alternately, they may discover that they hate being fat because they no longer feel (or fear they will not be perceived as) attractive. Many women who have never had food or weight problems first encounter them during pregnancy, when their body begins to enlarge, and they worry that they won't be able to take off the weight after the baby is born. Along with using therapy to discuss these fears, a nutritional consult can be enormously useful when clients are trying to get pregnant, during pregnancy, and after childbirth, especially if the client chooses to breastfeed.

Along with wanting to be healthy for and through a pregnancy, clients often are motivated to overcome eating problems when their children become toddlers. Aware that they have been eating dysfunctionally, many mothers believe that feeding their children will push them to become a better role model for "normal" eating. Some succeed in "doing it for their children." Others are fearful of being able to manage new and different foods in the house and wonder how they will nourish themselves along with another person. Many new parents are painfully tempted to share their children's food, such as macaroni and cheese, highly sweetened or "candy-rich" cereals, full-fat products, or peanut butter and jelly sandwiches. Parents may be too tired to prepare foods for themselves and end up eating things they would never cook for themselves or order on their own.

Sometimes Mom and Dad have no idea that their food choices are modeling negative behaviors for their children—until they are told by a doctor or teacher that a son or daughter is under- or overweight. If they are caring, mentally healthy parents, they can use the opportunity to change their eating habits along with their children's, but this may be a huge dilemma. Mom may sneak treats up to her room, or Dad may run out to have an ice cream or a Big Mac. Parents who are too calorie conscious and rigidly restrict their children's food selections and portion sizes may be thrown into a tailspin if children appear undernourished or underweight. They may find it nearly impossible to allow their children to eat what they want because they are so restricted themselves.

Parents may not realize that encouraging or pushing children to eat one way while eating another way sends a confusing double message that leads to an equally confusing double bind: should I eat like Mom or Dad whom I admire, or follow their food instructions? Therapy can be enormously helpful in pointing out these dilemmas to parents and helping them deal with their food problems so that they can support their children in becoming "normal" eaters. However, it is vital that parents work on changing their own habits for themselves as much as for their children. If they don't, there is a good chance they will revert to old, unhealthy patterns when their children get older.

Reflections for Therapist

1. What do I know about the client that makes me wonder if she may have difficulty with eating and weight during pregnancy?
2. What do I know about the client that makes me concerned that she may have difficulty with eating and weight during child-rearing?
3. What can we do now to prevent food and body problems from emerging during pregnancy? What can we do now to prevent food and body problems from surfacing after the child is born?
4. Does the client's partner need to be involved in discussions about eating and weight?
5. Would a nutritional consult be beneficial?

To help the client manage eating and weight problems during pregnancy and child-rearing, ask:

1. What are your concerns about eating and weight regarding pregnancy?
2. What are your concerns about eating and weight regarding child-rearing?
3. Do you understand the difference between "normal" and healthy eating?

4. Would a nutritional consult be helpful to you?

5. How can I help you feel better about food and weight as a parent?

Menopause

Female clients often complain about putting on weight due to menopause and shifting hormones. About 90% of menopausal women gain some weight between the ages of 35 and 55. Most will gain about 10 to 15 pounds, which will likely come on gradually, about 1 pound a year during perimenopause and more rapidly due to early or surgical menopause. Weight gain is due to fluctuating hormones, levels of estrogen, and testosterone, and androgen impacting appetite, metabolism, and fat ("Menopause and Weight Gain," Epigee Women's Health Web site).

Although women have come to associate (and often dread) menopause because of anticipated extra pounds, their eating habits and weight before menopause are a primary indicator of how their body will respond. A client's attitude depends largely on her body image (positive, negative, or neutral), her attitude toward fatness and thinness, and her sense of efficacy to control her life. For example, a woman who has maintained an average, comfortable weight for decades, or one who fears becoming fat, may cut back on calories and increase exercise when she notices the needle on the scale inching up during or after menopause, a healthy response.

A woman who has always struggled with weight might feel panicky about more weight gain with menopause, and equally despairing about being able to prevent it. If she has been dieting for decades without success, she is likely to feel frustrated, hopeless, and helpless to avoid weight gain. These feelings may lead to depression, increased appetite, decreased exercise, lowered self-esteem, and withdrawal from social activities. Telling a client at this point to eat less and get out and exercise more is like shouting at a deaf person: The client has already been there and done that. Sometimes a group can be useful, however, so that she can share frustrations with other women in a similar situation and get support and feedback on how to make and stay committed to important lifestyle changes.

Other women have never struggled with weight issues and are surprised and dismayed when menopause packs on pounds. Because they have always pretty much eaten what they wanted, they may not know what to do. Some may simply cut calories and exercise more and find they are able to minimize weight gain. Those who have prided themselves on thinness all their lives may have the most trouble adjusting and are most at risk for an eating disorder. These are women who start to trim calories and cannot stop or who turn to purging to stay slim.

Menopause also brings up body image issues for women because this time ends their fertile years, which some equate with being desirable, attractive, and sexual. They see menopause as the door to old age. Some will redouble their efforts to look good, while others will feel relief that they can finally stop caring so much about appearance. A few will let themselves go completely. Their problems may not be so much about food and weight, but about how they relate to their bodies in the second half of life.

Women may speak of menopause in a joking way and make cavalier comments about getting fat. They may truly not be concerned or this may be their way of raising a subject about which they are uncomfortable. Many women become depressed at "losing their looks" and believe that menopausal weight gain is inevitable, which is not necessarily true. They need help focusing on other positive qualities in themselves that are enduring and in making sure that going up a dress size does not change how they value themselves.

To help the client understand her food and body menopause-related concerns, ask:

1. Do you have concerns about eating and weight regarding menopause?
2. Because of menopause, what do you expect to happen regarding your appetite and body? Based on what evidence?
3. How are you feeling about possible weight gain (for example, resigned, in denial, upset)? What can you do to make your thinking more positive?
4. Would becoming part of a group of women dealing with menopause or seeing a nutritionist/dietician or exercise trainer help you?
5. How can we work together to support you going through menopause with positive feelings about food and your body?

Aging and Retirement

For some people retirement is a welcome relief and change of pace. After working for decades, they finally get to do what they *really* want—pursue avocations and hobbies, spend time with family and friends, travel, or simply kick back and relax. Other people miss the structure and hustle and bustle of a job or the challenges of a career and find they have too much time on their hands. Some folks do not change their eating very much as they age and will proudly tell you that they weigh just about what they did as a young man or woman. But most retirees find that as they become less active, more homebound, and at the mercy of a slowed-down, aging body, they put on weight more easily.

Many retirees overfocus on food because other interests have gradually dropped out of their lives. They are no longer working, friends and family members have died, and others live far away. With little to occupy their time, food shopping becomes a filler activity, as do cooking, eating, and cleaning up after a meal. Going out for breakfast, lunch, or dinner is an event, a bright spot in an otherwise boring day. Food becomes the all-purpose answer to what makes life worth living.

This attitude is hardly true of all senior retirees, but clients who have not adjusted well to retirement are at risk for centering their life around food and gaining weight. Elders who are circumscribed in their activities because they have difficulty getting around are also in danger of turning to eating as something to do. Moreover, if they are bored, unhappy, or lonely, food becomes a cheap, accessible, instant friend who is there to comfort and cheer them up. Elders who live in a retirement community or home may have access to walking paths and a health club, but many others are housebound without transportation or stuck in apartments or rooming houses with little access to exercise venues. Even if there were a gym or pool not too far away, many seniors no longer drive and would have no way of getting there. Some cannot get out as often as they would like because they reside in a rainy, cold, icy, or snowy climate. Additionally, many elders live in unsafe neighborhoods where it is hazardous to go out and take a walk, and some have such severe health problems that exercise is out of the question.

Finding an elder shuttle for a client might do the trick to get him out to a local mall with a walking club or to a senior center that has exercise classes. Sometimes we need to involve a physical therapist to teach the client at-home exercises for balance and flexibility. Chair exercises can be easily learned. It is important not to give up on these clients, many of whom are overweight and underexercised and have already given up on themselves. Even small changes can make a difference, and one tiny shift may lead to another.

Not every older person or retiree is susceptible to added pounds. For some, keeping weight on is a challenge. Many seniors cannot afford to eat nutritiously because they are on a fixed budget or because they end up spending most of their tiny income on medication and housing. Some are dependent on others to grocery-shop for them. Moreover, as people age and senses become less acute, they may lose their appetite and interest in eating. Eating may be painful due to gum disease, indigestion, or dental problems, such as missing teeth or poorly fitting dentures; with cognitive slippage and diseases like dementia, seniors may simply forget to eat.

When dealing with elderly clients, we must listen carefully for any mention of a shift in relationship to food. Diminished appetite may indicate pain, worsening heart failure, depression, dementia, or the beginnings of pneumonia. Our sharpest assessment skills are useful in flagging or diagnosing a problem, and therapy can be enormously helpful in supporting lifestyle changes. However, talk therapy alone is not always enough to help a client who is undernourished and underweight. The family generally should be notified and brought in to improve the feeding/eating situation, if possible. Effort must be made to contact friends and neighbors who might pitch in to grocery-shop or cook for the client. The client's doctor should be notified of a major weight decrease or significant loss of appetite. A case manager, home health aide, or nutritional consult might be useful. Encouraging the client to get an evaluation for medication (for depression or appetite stimulation) should also be a consideration.

Reflections for Therapist

1. What do I know about the client that makes me concerned she will have difficulty with body issues around menopause and as she ages?

2. What are her strengths that will help her deal with these issues?

3. What are the challenges and underlying conflicts that will work against her attempt to effectively resolve these issues?

4. What are the specific changes the client has to make?

5. Are there community resources that can help (for example, support groups, care agencies, nutritionists/dieticians) that need to be involved?

6. Do I need to contact the client's doctor or family members?

To help the client who has eating and weight issues related to aging, ask:

1. Have you lost or gained weight recently, especially since retirement?

2. Why do you think you are losing or gaining weight?

3. If you have lost weight, how is your appetite? What prevents you from eating? What would encourage you to eat more?

4. If you have gained weight, how has your appetite or exercise level changed?

5. What do you need more of in your life to stop focusing so much on food? What do you need less of?

6. Is there anyone who could help you make the changes you need in the food and weight arenas (for example, friends, relatives, neighbors)?

7. What could we do together that will help you stabilize your appetite and maintain a healthy weight?

Miscellaneous

There are other situations that also may produce changes in eating or concerns about weight. Naturally, any major shift in circumstance, especially beginnings, endings, crises, trauma, transitions, or major stressors such as moving, changing jobs, or losing or caring for a loved one can precipitate a shift in appetite. Some people who go through a crunch or stressful time continue to eat relatively normally and maintain a healthy weight. They may overeat for a while until their appetite returns to normal and the weight comes off, or undereat until their situation has stabilized and the desire for food returns. However, for folks who have had eating issues, stress is often a trigger for dysfunctional eating even after years or decades of maintaining a steady, comfortable weight and a positive relationship with food.

For example, weight may become a strong focus when individuals become heavily involved in competitive athletics. High school and college athletes are especially vulnerable to developing eating disorders. In a study done by Cornell University, 40% of male football players were found to engage in some form of disordered eating ("General Eating Disorder Fact Sheet," MEDA Web site). In a 2002 study of 425 female college athletes, 43% said they were terrified of being or becoming too heavy, and 55% reported experiencing pressure to achieve or maintain a certain weight. Some 2–3% of female college athletes have full-fledged, diagnosable eating disorders, which is about the same as the population as a whole (Hellmich, 2006). Naturally, someone who has struggled with eating at any time in her life might find that the problem recurs. But feeding issues also emerge for individuals who have never had an eating problem, but end up restricting or purging because they see other athletes doing it and believe they have to engage in unhealthy behaviors in order to compete.

Engaging in a stringent regime of slimming down, bulking up, or excessive practice can happen to anyone in the world of athletics or dance. Eating disorders are significant problems in ballet and other dance areas, figure skating, gymnastics, running, bicycling, swimming, rowing, horse racing, ski jumping, and riding. Even wrestlers may binge eat and load up on carbohydrates before a match, then purge to make weight in a lower class. Females endure a double whammy because of society's pressure to be slim combined with the need for slenderness in dance and low body weight in other sports.

Clients who are most at risk, at any age, are the ones who are highly competitive, more wrapped up in winning than in playing the game, suffering from low self-esteem, or employing all-or-nothing thinking. They may view disordered eating as the one and only way to get an edge on competitors and may deny or minimize how they are compromising their health by binge eating, purging, overexercising, or failing to nourish themselves properly. Helping driven clients like this overcome eating problems can be long and arduous work because the behavior is so ego syntonic and covertly (or sometimes, overtly) encouraged. Educating clients about the damage they are inflicting on their bodies and helping them establish other (less competitive) life goals are useful therapeutic avenues to explore. Occasionally, however, clients should be encouraged to drop out of sport or dance if they are unable to stop destructive eating behaviors that are endangering their health.

Another circumstance in which eating and weight concerns may surface is when clients stop smoking. Because nicotine elevates metabolism and quitting smoking causes it to return to its normal functioning, most people experience a 5-to-10- pound weight gain when they give up cigarettes. Moreover, nicotine is an oral habit and it is natural to turn to food as a substitute. For people who are not concerned about putting on a few pounds, weight gain may be only a minor consequence of shaking the smoking habit. However, for the "addictive personality," increased eating and weight gain occur more often than not.

For folks who use cigarettes to control their weight or panic over gaining a pound, quitting can be a very trying time. Not only do they feel deprived of cigarettes, but they know that if they turn to food instead, they are setting themselves up to feel deprived down the road when they want to reduce their food intake. Many clients, in fact, who say they would love to stop smoking do not because they fear that quitting will lead to weight gain. This is true even if they know that the weight will eventually come off. Encouraging clients to find other ways to cope with stress (like carbohydrates, nicotine relaxes us) is necessary, along with suggesting that quitters drink lots of fluids, chew gum, and suck on toothpicks until oral urges subside.

Most important is to help clients recognize that quitting smoking is a tremendously positive thing to do for their health and longevity (and the health of those who live with them) and to support them in not smoking even if their weight inches up. Aiding them in tolerating frustration, not giving in to impulse, and keeping them focused will go a long way toward sustaining their motivation. If they are able to avoid gaining weight while stopping smoking, all well and good. If not, we need to let them know that we will be there to help them start losing weight as soon as they are ready.

Another situation that may trigger change in appetite is when a client becomes a primary caregiver. This can happen at any age. A young mother may need to take care of a sick child, a middle-aged son may be responsible for the care of his aging parents, or an elderly person may end up attending to a failing spouse or sibling. In some cases, the client will turn to food to handle the increased stress, especially if she is stuck at home and has given up or decreased social activities. Other times, the caretaker is so exhausted that she is unable to eat and has little interest in or energy for preparing food for herself. Whenever clients becomes primary caretakers, it is a good idea to start thinking about how appetite and eating routines might change and adversely affect them.

To assess if the client is vulnerable to changes in weight or appetite, ask:

1. Is there anything going on in your life that makes you more or less inclined to eat, especially transitions or change in quality of life?
2. When under stress, how do you take care of yourself other than with food?
3. When you are in crisis, are you likely to eat more or less?
4. If you smoke, do you want to quit? If so, does the thought of gaining weight put you off?
5. Are you engaged in any competitive sports or activities that make you want to lose weight or rigidly control your eating?
6. How can I help you make sure that you are eating healthily and staying fit?

Eating and weight issues may emerge suddenly due to life changes or gradually over the years. Our goal is to help clients identify when they are troubled by food and when they are getting into trouble by becoming over- or underweight. It is also important for them to know that if they have had eating problems in the past, there is a good chance that stressful circumstances will trigger food issues again. As we get to know clients, we can encourage them to think ahead when major change is about to happen—divorce, retirement, childbirth, loss of a parent, or a move across the country—to anticipate if food and weight concerns will return and how they might deal with them.

CHAPTER 9

Nutrition
and Fitness

A ny time we raise the topics of eating and weight with clients, we can be pretty sure that questions about nutrition and fitness will follow. How can we talk about eating without discussing which foods pack the most nutritional punch and which will speed us down the road to serious illness? How can we speak of weight without talking exercise, heart health, disease prevention, and longevity? We cannot avoid these areas, but that does not mean we need to know everything about them. Instead, we can get discussion rolling, then involve other professionals in supporting clients in reaching nutritional and fitness goals.

Although clients might pressure us, or we might feel pressured, to address nutrition hand in hand with eating problems, it is often beneficial to postpone discussion until we thoroughly understand what is going wrong with a client's eating. Are we dealing with a pregnant woman who has always had a comfortable relationship with food who is now so overly focused on eating "right" for the fetus that she no longer enjoys it? Are we working with an elderly widower whose wife used to cook lavish meals for him who now feels condemned to eating frozen dinners for the rest of his life? If so, discussion about nutrition might be useful but, obviously, that is not all that is needed. We must determine whether the pregnant client is trying to be a perfect mother-to-be in order to produce a perfect child, and whether the widower is depressed and in need of companionship and social connections as well as tasty dinners.

The rule of thumb for working with clients with major eating issues is to help them become "normal" eaters before focusing on nutrition. This may take months or, occasionally, years. Of course, this does not mean avoiding mention of healthy versus unhealthy foods or refusing to discuss the kinds and amounts of food clients eat. Do they eat only junk food or health food? Do they generally overeat or undereat? Or, do they alternate between eating only organic and macrobiotic foods and foods that are unhealthy? It does mean waiting until clients are eating "normally" fairly consistently for many months before changing the focus of discussion to consuming healthier foods.

Here's why. When disordered eaters focus on eating "right" or healthily, they often (unconsciously or consciously) restrict their choices, believing they *should* be eating by the book, and end up reacting as if they are on a diet. Restriction for any reason causes them to feel deprived, which often leads to rebelling by eating "unhealthy" foods. Rather than direct clients to eat salads, vegetables, and whole grains, it is better to support them in intuitive eating: helping them identify their hunger level and what they are in the mood for; encouraging them to stay aware while eating and stop eating when full; and teaching them how to deal with emotions without abusing food.

A word here about *intuitive* or *normal* eating. For our purposes, the terms are interchangeable and promote an approach to eating that is body-centered. Eating is intuitive, or instinctive, because it is based primarily on innate body signals about hunger, cravings, and satiation. It is considered normal because this is how the standard-issue human body is programmed to keep the species alive—to eat when hungry, make satisfying food choices, eat with awareness and enjoyment, and stop when full or satisfied. However, because eating is intuitive does not mean that it precludes using our brains to abet our instincts. Nor does *normal* mean that every bite must be for the betterment of self or humankind. Normal eaters eat a wide range of foods.

We must have a thorough understanding of the difference between normal and healthy eating in order to help clients. That means recognizing that intuitive or normal eaters are not necessarily nutritious eaters and that nutritious eaters may eat neither normally nor from instinct. Ideally, of course, each of us (clinician and client alike) would eat intuitively *and* healthily most of the time, but pressures to be thin and to follow strict nutrition guidelines coupled with an abundance of accessible, delicious foods makes that a (pardon the pun) pie-in-the-sky goal. Food, eating, and weight have taken on such a life of their own in present culture that sometimes the best any of us can be is a work in progress.

Clients with eating problems will have a range of information about and interest in nutrition and exercise. A few might be relatively close to "normal" eaters, but remain relatively ignorant about what foods have health value and what foods do not. A handful of couch potatoes might find that, in spite of eating "normally" and fairly nutritiously, with advancing years they need to engage in some or more exercise. Others might know a good deal about nutrition and exercise faithfully, but be chronic over- or undereaters. Some will be as expert about healthy eating as a dietician or spend hours exercising, but still alternate dieting by the book with binge eating. By far the largest group will be those who have difficulty maintaining an ongoing exercise program and who do not, on the whole, follow nutrition guidelines.

For clients who are more or less "normal" eaters, but lack information about nutrition, the wisest thing to do is to refer them to a registered dietician or certified nutritionist (make certain the professional is licensed and experienced) while you continue to talk about their food concerns. Maybe they have recently received a promotion and are now constantly traveling for work and eating out a lot. While you discuss the stress (or distress) this change in eating has generated—the clients might be anxious about succeeding in their new position and may be fixating on eating rather than experiencing their angst—a dietician can help them choose satisfying foods and master a knack for eating well down the road.

A pregnant teenager who is eager to have a healthy baby and afraid of gaining too much weight might have no clue how to read labels, and a nutritionist may help her understand what all that tiny print on food packaging actually means. A client who never had weight problems might need guidance about what to eat after colon cancer surgery or being diagnosed with Crohn's disease or celiac disease, food allergies, or irritable bowel syndrome. Elderly clients who have been losing weight steadily and have little interest in food might benefit from learning what they must eat to stay healthy and finding out about nutritional supplements.

On the exercise front, it is crucial to make sure that clients who intend to begin any kind of program are in good enough health; some may even need to get medical clearance before beginning an exercise regime. Although most healthy clients can get away with not visiting a doctor, anyone with serious medical problems or who is postsurgery, elderly, or pregnant should, especially if they have any history of cardiovascular disease. While we all have our share of clients who need to be prodded to buy a gym membership or take a walk, there are also clients who suddenly become gung ho for exercise and may endanger themselves if they are not careful.

There are many avenues that could lead to discussion about exercise. A divorced or widowed client who is thinking about dating and getting into shape might be guided toward joining a health club—not only to become fit but to make friends and social contacts. A middle-aged man recovering from a heart attack who has never run for a bus or lifted a barbell would benefit tremendously by getting advice from a trainer, privately or at a gym. A couple trying to spend more time with each other might achieve their intimacy goals—and stay fit—by taking time out to learn a sport together (bicycling, skiing, tennis, bowling), by joining a dance class, or by doing yard work or household chores together.

Along with advising clients to see a licensed professional for nutritional counseling, it is equally important to steer clients toward reputable health and fitness facilities and athletic trainers and fitness coaches who have the skill level, experience, and training to know what they are doing. The last thing we want is to have a client injured while she is trying to get into shape! It is excellent assertiveness training for clients who are joining a gym to ask about the expertise and availability of staff and to inquire about credentials, experience, and references when hiring a trainer or coach.

Although we should not expect to be experts in nutritional counseling or exercise physiology (it is hard enough to stay current on psychological issues!), it helps to have a basic grounding in these two areas. This is all clients generally need from us as they explore their eating and weight concerns. We can always read books and go online, if necessary, to expand our knowledge about healthy eating and fitness. Again, with so much conflicting information on the Internet, we must separate out reputable Web sites from those that are trying to sell products.

There are hundreds of books on nutrition, but not all are based on good science. Some are the experiences of one person, include only anecdotal or unproven evidence, or are based on pseudoscience. The same is true of Web sites on which a person gives her opinion of what is healthy and unhealthy to eat, and on which companies push products (such as food, supplements, medications, and diet plans). Our best bet is to refer to books by well regarded, credentialed dieticians, medical doctors, and scientists; the most up-to-date information may be found on the Web sites and in the newsletters of nutrition schools (for example, Tufts University, Johns Hopkins, the University of California at Berkeley, as well as most government Web sites, especially the U.S. Department of Public Health).

There are also fitness Web sites that are trying to sell products, usually aerobics videos or exercise machines, which may not give the whole story on exercise and may even make false claims. Again, we should seek out Web sites and books whose legitimacy comes from science and licensed professionals, especially those who have good standing in their fields and a sound track record. Remember, giving clients the wrong information can often be worse than giving them no information at all.

Reflections for Therapist

1. How close is the client to being a "normal," intuitive eater?
2. How motivated is the client to exercise, eat "normally," or eat nutritiously? What might increase her motivation?
3. Would physical therapy or a nutritional or exercise consult help motivate her?
4. What issues need to be addressed and resolved before the client is ready for a consultation?

To assess client motivation and goals in the areas of motivation and fitness, ask:

1. What are your eating goals? weight goals? nutritional goals? fitness goals?
2. What is a reasonable amount of time for you to reach each of these goals?

3. How would you assess your motivation in each area (high-medium-low)?
4. What obstacles do you identify in reaching each of these goals?
5. How could we work together to remove these obstacles and improve your incentives?

Nutrition

Food

Whether or not we follow nutritional eating guidelines ourselves, most of us know the basics by now: eat more fruits, vegetables, and whole grains, avoid transfats and foods high in bad cholesterol, and keep sweets and treats to a minimum. This advice has stood the dual tests of science and time and sounds suspiciously like what our grandparents might have practiced and told us regarding eating simply and in moderation.

In our work with clients, it helps to have a more comprehensive body of knowledge to draw from, especially as this information is more or less at our fingertips thanks to the World Wide Web. However, sometimes it seems as if the recommendations we find for foods, supplements, vitamins, and minerals change more rapidly than we can follow. We go along for decades believing that potatoes are wholesome and good for us, then discover they are right up there on the glycemic index and that we should eat them sparingly. Same goes for eggs, which many of us were taught contained good-quality protein—until we learned that eggs were high in bad cholesterol and then, in a turnabout, that they are not so harmful after all. The biggest debates have been between diets that promote consumption of red meat and fat and others that consider them the primary cause of heart disease and premature death. Then there are the questions about the benefits of eating organic or raw foods only, the hazards of products that are genetically modified, and whether to pursue a vegetarian or vegan lifestyle.

An excellent, commonsense, well-received book about food is *What to Eat* by Marion Nestle, professor of nutrition at New York University (Nestle, 2006). She does as good a job as anyone explaining the nuts and bolts of healthy eating and musts and myths of nutrition, although she is right up front in saying that most adult Americans do not follow dietary guidelines. Another excellent resource is MyPyramid.gov, the Web site of the U.S. Department of Agriculture (USDA), which presents and explains the food guide Pyramid released in 2005. Based on a 2,000-calorie diet, it recommends that adults consume daily:

- at least 6 ounces of whole grains in the form of rice, crackers, cereal, bread, or pasta, half of which are whole grain and half of which are refined;
- 2–3 cups of vegetables divided into categories of dark green, starchy, orange, other, and dry beans and peas;
- 2 cups of fruit, but go easy on fruit juices;
- 3 cups of milk or milk products, including cheese and yogurt; and
- 5.5 ounces of lean meat, chicken, fish, and beans.

The site describes the differences in types of oils and goes into detail about varieties of fruits and vegetables. It also talks about "discretionary" calories, or those that we should keep to a minimum, that is, foods that are high-calorie and/or high-fat, and the need to limit salt. Although the site is a bit difficult to navigate, it does move away from the one-size-fits-all nutritional plan of yesteryear and offers a more individualized approach based on gender, age, weight, height, and physical-activity level. It also provides information for a number of ethnic/cultural groups, including Latin American, Native American, Asian, and Mediterranean.

The explanation of a serving size is a bit confusing and may range from a half cup to a cup, a slice, a piece, 2 tablespoons, or 2–8 ounces, depending on the food. The site does give a great many examples and most folks should be able to get the hang of what a serving is with practice—or they can always refer back to the Web pages. This is only one site among many with a wealth of solid information on nutrition and to which we can refer clients who want to learn more about healthy eating.

The problem with this information is that it actually can promote or reinforce disordered eating by asking that clients measure and weigh food and think about the number of calories they contain. To the ears of disordered eaters, the food pyramid sounds suspiciously like a diet. The trick is to help clients see it as a basis for making choices and not as a way to obsess about food and deny themselves pleasure. The food pyramid and accessing nutritional information is most helpful to clients who truly have no idea about the number of calories or amount of fat and salt they consume in a day. Some are positively shocked to hear how many grams of fat there are in a Big Mac or a Whopper or how calorie-laden a Frapuccino is.

The best approach for clients is not to count calories or fat grams but to focus on eating to feed their cells effectively. Better that they consider whether a food will nourish their body than how fat or thin it will make them. This change of viewpoint is crucial if clients are to create a positive relationship with food and maintain a comfortable weight for life. The truth is, much of this change can be generated by how we as clinicians approach the subject, that is, whether we focus on fatness and thinness or health and fitness.

Dietary Supplements

Also known as micronutrients, vitamins and minerals are "substances [the] body needs in small but steady amounts for normal growth, function and health" ("Dietary Supplements: Using Vitamin and Mineral

Supplements Wisely," Mayo Clinic Web site). Because the body cannot make most micronutrients, we must get them from food or dietary supplements. There is nothing wrong with taking supplements, and in some cases, they are essential to health and well-being, but the general consensus is that it is better to get nutrients from food. Some folks believe that if they take vitamins and minerals, they can afford to fudge a healthy diet. They live on junk food and pretend that they are not compromising their health because they swallow handfuls of supplements daily. They *are* better off supplementing their poor diets in this way, but are still endangering themselves by making ongoing unhealthy food choices.

Vitamins are needed for growth, digestion, and nerve function. They are involved in many biological processes, including enabling the body to use carbohydrates, fats, and protein for energy and to repair cell damage. Most vitamins have multiple functions, but do not themselves contain calories. Vitamins can be either water-soluble or fat-soluble.

Water-soluble vitamins are easily absorbed by the body and are not stored in large amounts by the body. They include vitamin B1/thiamine, B2/riboflavin, B3/niacin, B5/pantothenic acid, B6/pyrionxine, B12/cyanocobalamin, C/ascorbic acid, H/biotin, and Folic Acid (folate).

Fat soluble vitamins are stored in body fat and are pulled out of storage, so to speak, when they are needed. They include vitamin A/retinoids, D/calciferol, E/tocopherol, and K/naphthoquinone.

Minerals are the primary components of bones and teeth as well as the building blocks of cells and enzymes. They help regulate fluid balance and the movement of nerve impulses, and they deliver oxygen to cells and carry carbon dioxide away from them. The most important minerals include Calcium, Iodine, Iron, Magnesium, Phosphorous, and Zinc.

Because the requisite amount of vitamins and minerals varies in many cases according to gender, age, and other conditions (such as pregnancy and menopause), it is impossible to provide general information about an individual client's actual needs. This information is readily available through books and on the Internet. Clients should be encouraged to acquire this information on their own, when possible, and bring it into therapy for discussion. It is important, especially for clients who tend to be disorganized or overwhelmed, or who frequently "forget" or lapse for long periods of time in their self-care duties, to explore how they feel about taking supplements and come up with a plan to help them stay motivated and committed.

During a crisis or in times of stress—when a client's body is most in need of nutrients—may be exactly when she becomes over-whelmed, depressed, and anxious, eats poorly, and gives up taking supplements. This is a sign of stress itself, leading to poor self-care, and she may need help recommitting to getting her daily doses and may respond well to periodic check-ins about them. Clients who have an all-or-nothing perspective tend to take supplements for a while, when they are on the upswing, and stop taking them (along with ceasing other beneficial activities such as exercising and sleeping and eating well) as they start to backslide or become more depressed.

To help the client assess knowledge about and motivation to take vitamins, ask:

1. Do you regularly take vitamins? If so, how long have you been doing so? If not, why not?
2. What motivates you to take them?
3. What makes you stop taking them?
4. How do you think not taking them affects your health?
5. How can we work together to keep you on track?
6. Do you need a consult with a dietician or nutritionist who can help you figure out what vitamins and minerals to take?

Fitness

There was a time when exercise was not a multibillion-dollar industry, but was meant to provide enjoyment—think skating, bowling, swimming, sledding, softball, and bike riding—and get our blood moving. Now, although it still brings pleasure to some, it is more often viewed as an activity to check off on a daily or weekly to-do list. Sadly, for many folks, exercise has become yet another self-care chore on a list that seems to grow longer by the year. Exercise, which used to be thought of as a fun way to pass the time, is now considered work because we have attached the goal of fitness to it.

What exactly is fitness? It is generally defined as the attributes that people have or achieve relating to their ability to perform physical activity. Talking about fitness with clients can be dicey and delicate, a subject on which we may need to tread lightly. Along with "healthy eating," it is another one of those must-do activities that may cause clients to either feel proud when they do it or ashamed when they do not. The subject is complicated by the fact that some clients appear healthy because they throw themselves into getting into shape, when the truth is that they are addicted to exercise to avoid distressing feelings and may be damaging their bodies in the process.

Some clients with food problems will bring up the desire to be fit and to exercise, while others will want to focus only on changing their eating habits and ignore this aspect of physical well-being. Most understand the health benefits of exercise, but many consider it merely a way to lose weight. A large number will have tried exercise programs and dropped out, coming to us with a history of failure they do not completely understand and fear repeating. As always, we need to start where the client is, which may be helping them view exercise as part of a broader goal of being fit and healthy, being honest about how committed they are to these goals, and exploring underlying self-care conflicts that make clients sabotage health gains.

According to most experts, there are five basic components of physical fitness: cardiorespiratory endurance, muscular strength, muscular endurance, flexibility, and body composition. All are equally important to physical health. The U.S. Department of Health and Human services cites the following requirements for fitness ("Components of Phsyical Fitness," U.S. Department of Health and Human Services Web site).

Cardiorespiratory Endurance: The ability of the body's circulatory and respiratory systems to supply fuel during sustained physical activity, to deliver oxygen and nutrients to tissues, and to remove wastes. This kind of endurance is increased by keeping the heart rate elevated at a safe level for a sustained period of time. Walking, swimming, skating, skiing, and bicyling are activities that build cardiorespiratory endurance.

Muscular Strength: The ability of muscle to exert force during an activity. In order to strengthen muscles, they must work against resistance. Using weights, elastic bands, medicine balls, and exercise machines such as a stairstepper all build muscular strength.

Muscular Endurance: The ability of the muscle to continue to perform without fatigue. Walking, jogging, bicycling, and dancing are activities that build muscular endurance.

Body Composition: The relative amount of muscle, fat, bone, and other vital parts of the body.

Flexibility: The range of motion around a joint. Good joint flexibility is a must to prevent injury. Exercises that increase flexibility are stretching, swimming, and yoga.

In addition to these five basic components, physical fitness also includes the following (from "Components of Fitness," Sports Coach Brian Mac's Web site):

Power: "The ability to exert maximum muscular contraction

instantly in an explosive burst of movements. The two facets of power are strength and speed (for example, jumping or starting a sprint)."

Agility: "The ability to perform a series of explosive power movements in rapid succession in opposing directions (for example, zigzag running or cutting movements)."

Balance: "The ability to control the body's position, either stationary (for example, doing a handstand) or while moving (for example, performing a gymnastics stunt)."

Coordination: "The ability to integrate the above-listed components so that effective movements are achieved."

There are numerous reasons that clients cite for not exercising or not doing it consistently enough to achieve benefit, including not having the time, lacking money to join a health facility, fear of injury or damaging health (common in people who have had heart problems), doubting that they will stay motivated and continue (often based on previous experience), believing that getting fit is too hard, fear of and shame about wearing workout clothes in public (this reason surfaces most frequently with clients who are overweight, and sometimes with clients who are underweight), feeling overwhelmed by all the effort ahead, and not knowing how to get started.

It is true that some clients have very little time for formal exercise—they may be raising a family and already have two (or three) jobs. It is also a fact that health clubs are expensive. However, studies have shown that people can gain physical benefits from informal exercise such as walking, raking leaves, cleaning house, taking out the dog, and playing touch football with the kids. Making lifestyle changes such as climbing stairs rather than taking an elevator and walking or bicycling to work rather than driving all help get a body moving and into shape.

Although one of the ways to engage clients in becoming more fit is through their desire to achieve or sustain a particular weight, it may not be the one with the most sticking power. In general, those clients who are serious about exercise—other than those who are compulsive—are doing it as much (or more) for its health benefits as to get or stay trim. These people have a strong, ongoing commitment to care for themselves the best they can. Explaining how exercise can improve the quality of life for clients both physically and mentally can go a long way toward improving clients' motivation and commitment to exercise.

Health Benefits

WebMD cites the following health benefits for regular exercise ("The Incredible Benefits of Regular Exercise," WebMD Web site).

- Healthy weight: Regular exercise helps use up oxygen, causes the body to burn stored fat and, therefore, reduce fat stores. It creates muscle, which burns more calories than fat (even when the body is at rest), so that there is a two-for-one positive effect.
- Strong bones: Weight-bearing activities such as walking, running, dancing, handball, and resistance training build bone mass and keep muscles strong.
- Better skin: By improving circulation and the delivery of nutrients to skin, regular exercise helps remove toxins or poisons from the body. Circulating oxygen to the skin also gives it a more "alive" color and increases the production of collagen, the connective tissue that plumps skin and reduces the appearance of wrinkles.
- Reduced stress: Regular exercise reduces the production of stress hormones that can be harmful to the body. Instead, activity causes muscles to relax as the body reduces its heart rate and decreases blood pressure.
- Improved mood: Ongoing exercise can be a real mood booster. It reduces symptoms of moderate depression by releasing endorphins, the brain chemicals that produce happy, positive feelings, and by increasing production of serotonin, a neurotransmitter that is a mood calmer and natural antianxiety chemical.
- Stronger immune system: Regular exercise bolsters the immune

system, which may result in reducing viral activity in the body, such as colds and flu.

- Better brain power: Exercise generates blood flow to the brain, helping it receive oxygen and nutrients that are necessary for clear and quick thinking.
- Disease prevention: The best news about regular exercise may be in disease prevention and increased longevity. Staying active helps lessen the chest pain of angina and symptoms of coronary artery disease, decreases heart attack risk, delays the onset of type 2 diabetes and helps in diabetes management, lowers the risk of developing Parkinson's disease, may help prevent breast, colon, and other types of cancer, and may delay the onset of Alzheimer's disease.

Clients often wonder about and ask how much exercise they need on a regular basis to maintain a healthy weight and stay fit. Although there has been disagreement among experts in the past, the current rule of thumb is to shoot for mild exercise at moderate intensity for at least 30 minutes a day. The exercise does not need to be done all at one time and can be broken up into 10-minute spurts; in fact, the latest thinking is that sporadic exercise promotes greater physical benefit than doing it all at once. Nor need exercise be "formal," such as using a weight machine or attending an aerobics class. The best exercise program is one that clients will continue to do that targets endurance, flexibility, strength, and balance.

In the area of exercise—as in nutrition—it works best to do what we know best, which is supporting clients in reaching their goals. That means helping them clarify their fitness objectives, identify the kinds of activities they enjoy and believe they will stay motivated to do, recognize health conditions that would make exercise difficult or prohibitive, and work through unconscious ambivalence they have about exercise (related to money, time, body image, etc.). Sometimes our role is to act as a cheerleader and encourage clients to call friends to form a walking group, head to the park with their dog for a run, or take advantage of a membership special being run at a local gym.

Our job is to ferret out clients' unconscious reasons for not exercising. They may be out of touch with their emotions and may not understand that starting and stopping exercise over and over means that they probably have conflicting feelings about getting or staying in shape. Most clients are in touch with *manifest* beliefs and feelings that they should exercise but are out of touch with *latent* ones about why they do not want to. Often they are surprised at how these unconscious reasons keep them stuck. A word of caution: We have to be careful not to play out the positive side of their ambivalence and encourage them to "get over" negative feelings. It is their job to sort out their internal conflicts and come to a decision about exercising; they are the ones who must make the choice and live with its consequences.

If a client starts an exercise regime and begins to slack off, it is vital to raise the subject and ask what happened. The client may feel ashamed, but we must teach them that unlocking an underlying conflict is the only way to health. They need to grasp that *their intent is not aligned with their behavior,* which means that something unconscious is preventing them from staying on track. When they stop exercising, they may try to place us in the role of "monitor" or "parent," hoping we will be the force to "make" them resume. Our best bet is to process what is going on in the relationship and dig under the exercise issue for other dilemmas about dependence, self-care, and motivation.

To help the client recognize beliefs and feelings about exercise and fitness, ask:

1. Do you exercise regularly? If so, what do you do, for how long, and how often? If you don't exercise, why not?
2. What are your honest (perhaps mixed) feelings about exercising?
3. What is your reason for exercising (for example, health,

fitness, to lose weight, believing you should)? Is this enough to keep you motivated?

4. If you slack off or stop exercising after a period of time, why do you think this happens? What is the longest you've maintained a regular exercise program?

5. What obstacles are in the way of exercising? What would increase your commitment and motivation? What needs to change in your life to keep this commitment?

6. How can we work together to keep you exercising regularly?

7. Would a trainer help you start exercising or keep you motivated?

Weight

Supporting clients in establishing weight goals is not as simple as it may sound. They may have a realistic or unrealistic view of what they desire to weigh and we also may have our own (conscious and unconscious) opinions. This is true whether a client is under-, over-, or of average weight. That is, an underweight client might want to remain considerably below what might be healthy for her, a middle-aged overweight client might want to get down to the unachievable weight he was in high school, and an average-weight client who appears healthy might want to lose weight when she does not need to because she thinks she is fat.

For client and therapist alike, it is nearly impossible to identify an individual's "correct" weight. Doctors and the media tell us one thing while our bodies may tell us another. The best we can do is explore why clients want to be a particular weight and what is wrong with being higher or lower. Frequently clients want to return to a previous weight. However, if they have been overweight since childhood, they may have absolutely no idea what weight would be comfortable for their particular body (which may very likely be different from what weight charts say). A helpful approach is to suggest that the weight that will work best for them is the one they can easily maintain when they are eating "normally," have an active lifestyle, and are exercising regularly.

An important digression: We may sometimes have clients who are unable to do traditional exercise due to poor health or physical limitations. In this case, they should consult a doctor, a trainer, or a physical therapist to find out what they *can* do. Just because they cannot do everything that other people do does not mean that it is healthy for them to do nothing. For example, they can do chair or isometric exercises, use elastic bands, or swim.

As underweight clients put on a few pounds and overweight ones take them off, it will be necessary to help them revise their goals. It is common for clients to over- or underestimate what is possible by picking a number they wish to be and forcing their bodies to get there. Those who are too thin may not realize what a Herculean emotional effort it will take to gain weight and tolerate feeling full and "fat." Those who are heavy may be misled by rapid initial weight loss, only to find that they slow down fairly soon or reach a plateau. A healthy view is that putting on and taking off weight is going to be far more difficult than expected, both physically and psychologically.

Balancing out talking about nutrition and fitness with discussions on "normal" eating makes for a well-rounded approach to health and well-being. Most clients enjoy being educated—they perceive it as being given to—and psychoeducation is often a welcome break from the grueling work of digging up the past, straightening out the present, and preparing for the future. As always, we must take our lead from the client, neither forcing information on them nor failing to provide it when the time is right.

CHAPTER 10

Transference and Countertransference

It has been a long time since therapists were encouraged to be blank slates on which clients were meant to project their thoughts and feelings, to be dispassionate and neutral so that our egos would not get in the way of clients revealing themselves. Now, more often than not, we strive to be real people—warm and caring, humorous, imperfect, engaging, and as human as possible. We recognize and anticipate that a client will have reactions to us, transferential and otherwise, and that we might even get more mileage out of the relationship, particularly in community mental health work, by making ourselves more, rather than less, approachable. Most of us greatly prize our privacy and still choose not to self-disclose unless it is a last resort and there is no other way to deepen a connection or further the therapy. Our work continues to be based on getting to know every inch of the clients while they, often in great frustration, know barely a thing about our nonclinical selves.

Not surprisingly, clients frequently come to us with issues much like our own. After all, at rock bottom, many of the problems we encounter and treat stem merely from being human. Our kinship with clients works both ways. As wounded healers, because we have "been there," we know where they "are at," which helps us empathize with and understand their travails. On the other hand, cutting too close to the bone may stir up our unwanted and/or unresolved issues and deter us from bonding with clients and guiding them effectively through their difficulties.

Clients often do not realize that we may understand the specifics of their situations too well—how often are we uneasily viewed as mind readers?—because we have had the same or similar thoughts and feelings. We have suffered from depression, had children who misbehave, know the grief of losing a parent, regret past deeds and words, worry about fitting in and being loved, are recovering from addictions, have gone through divorce, agonize over decisions, or struggle with our tempers. Occasionally we may share information about ourselves to move the therapy forward, or clients may know particulars about our lives because we live in a small community or travel in the same social circle. However, for the most part, we are able to keep our "stuff" private and out of the therapeutic hour.

The secret nature of our issues generally remains true even if we have a problem with disordered eating. If we are thin, clients may assume we are blessed with a fast metabolism or that we have little interest in food. They may think, "Oh, she doesn't have to worry about putting on weight." If we are average weight, they may presume that we have a reasonably good relationship with food. In either case, how would they know if we starve ourselves all week only to binge-eat all weekend, how could they guess that we spend hours in the gym burning off the calories we overate (or believed we overate), or why would they suspect that we purge to keep ourselves slim or to prevent ourselves from becoming fat?

Although we can keep hidden almost every aspect of our lives— and certainly most of our problems—our weight is an open secret. Clients may ascribe our thinness to lucky genetics, but if we are heavy, they will probably think we have an eating problem. Not that our size should necessarily intrude into our work—unless, of course, we are dealing with a client who has eating and/or weight problems. Odds are that as clinicians, we have had little, if any, reason to think about our body size during sessions: We do our jobs well and that is all that matters to us and the client. Even working with clients who have food problems, it may not occur to us that our size might play a part in the clinical hour. After all, we think, we know how to help people; why should how we look matter? Perhaps it should not, but it often does.

Many clients with eating or weight problems will not care what shape we are—or are in—as long as we can help them. They may have reactions to us, even transferential ones, that have nothing to do with our size. Others might have concerns about our being undersized or oversized, but be embarrassed (for us or themselves) to talk about them. Moreover, their reactions may be either positive or negative or a mix. Our job is to be aware that clients may have feelings and assumptions about our weight so that we can explore them.

Client responses may be from ignorance, projection, or transference. For example, a client may see us as overweight and not be aware of how fit we are or that we are plump due to medication. A client who prizes thinness might project her own fears about fat onto us if we are large and assume we hate our size as much as she would if she looked like us. A client struggling with his weight might take an instant dislike to us based on our slim physique because his fitness-fanatic father still berates him for not getting out and exercising.

As if helping clients identify their issues and sort out their reactions to us were not enough, we, of course, have to deal with our own potential feelings about *their* size and shape. Our responses, too, are subject to ignorance, projection, and transference. If we struggle with slimming down and feeling attractive, we may take an instant dislike to a client who looks effortlessly slim and striking, as if she has stepped out of *Vogue* or he off the cover of *GQ*, or we may feel relieved when a client is fatter than we are. If we are naturally thin, we may feel repulsed by a morbidly obese client in spite of liking him enormously.

For better or worse, how the therapist feels about her body—and everyone else's—often works its way into the therapy when issues of weight are on the table. For example, it may be fairly easy to raise the subject of how a client seems to compete with us for airtime (and subsequently discover that we remind her of an overbearing, drama-queen sibling). It is far more difficult if we are heavy to bring up the subject of her being abusive to us in the same way she was nasty to her overweight sister who received all the parental fussing while she was ignored. By raising this issue, the therapist is drawing attention to her (less than perfect) body, which may be necessary for the client's growth, but which may make the clinician feel vulnerable and exposed.

What about how we are reeled back into the past when a client's life brings to mind our fat childhood among slim siblings, our health-fanatic father, our overweight mother who refused to go out in public or who caused us enormous embarrassment when she did, our secret eating when our parents battled nightly, or the teasing and ridicule we suffered because we were too overweight to join in neighborhood or schoolyard games? Dealing with clients who have weight problems at either extreme necessitates an examination of our cultural biases about food and weight and may require that we dig deeply into our own troubled past. It brings us right up against our current struggles with food and weight.

There are a number of potential scenarios that may occur between therapist and client in the weight and food arenas:

- therapist and client are overweight;
- therapist and client are underweight;
- therapist is overweight and client is underweight;
- therapist is underweight and client is overweight;
- therapist is average weight and client is either over- or underweight;
- therapist has an eating, but not a weight, problem and is treating a disordered eater.

These are broad descriptions of interactional possibilities that are meant to illuminate issues rather than provide an exact snapshot of what goes on between therapist and client. Although many clients come to us fat or thin, a substantial number have yo-yoing weights. They may currently have no weight problem, but still eat in a disordered fashion, or they may have the same large or small body size we have but have been at the other extreme at other times in their lives.

Reflections for Therapist

1. Has my eating or weight ever been an issue for me in treating a client?
2. Has my weight ever been an issue for a client?
3. How aware am I of prejudices I have about people who are fat or thin? What are those prejudices?
4. What are my preconceived notions about people with eating problems?
5. How might my weight or eating issues surface in treating clients with similar problems?
6. What kind of transference and countertransference do I usually run into with clients (for example, they sometimes see me as aloof, I often want to fix them, etc.)?

Overweight Therapist and Client

When both therapist and client are overweight, a number of client reactions are possible. She may feel an instant bond with us and expect that we will automatically understand her struggles. She may assume that our eating problems and attitude toward our body are exactly like hers. Most likely the client will be enormously relieved that she will not be judged for her size. Unfortunately, many clients with weight issues either avoid therapy or come and talk about everything but this problem because they are terrified that they will be looked down upon and be made to feel bad.

A client who hates and is ashamed of being fat may assume that we share her body perspective. She may have low self-esteem and a poor body image and be unable to imagine that a heavy person could feel anything but terrible about herself. Finding a therapist who is large may open the door to her sharing her self-contempt and self-disappointment in a way that she could not do (or at least not do early on) with a slimmer clinician. Whether the therapist actually shares the same negative body attitudes as the client is initially immaterial. The client feels mirrored by virtue of seeing a likeness of herself in a person she perceives as competent and powerful, which is often all that is needed to put her at ease.

It is equally possible that an overweight client might meet with a heavy therapist and feel instant concern or even panic that she will be unable to receive effective treatment. She might think that the therapist has nothing to offer because she does not know how to fix her own weight problems. Clients with weight problems who are fat phobic, thin obsessed, and stuck in the diet mentality often have tremendous contempt for large people in general and themselves in particular, and the therapist will be no exception. The client may feel disgusted by and contemptuous of the therapist and angry about being stuck with someone so incompetent—all this without the clinician saying a word!

On the other side are the feelings that the heavy clinician has treating an overweight client. If the therapist is comfortable with her body, she may be able to use humor and skill to bond, explore issues, and do what is necessary, if desired, to help her client reach eating and weight goals. *It is vital to remember that it is not crucial that we resolve our problems in order to help clients resolve theirs.* Most of us know this adage to be true. The key to a successful therapeutic relationship is recognizing our issues, staying in touch with our feelings, and using them to further treatment. In fact, it is entirely possible that an overweight clinician can help an overweight client lose weight and still not lose a pound herself.

It is also possible that a large therapist may wish to avoid the subject or feel inadequate to provide effective help. If she feels ashamed of her body or her inability to slim down, she may minimize the client's distress about weight or ignore cries for help. She may feel so hopeless about helping herself that she believes she has nothing to offer a client with eating problems. Or she may go overboard trying to fix her client because she feels so incompetent changing herself. She might think: I can help someone find a comfortable weight, even if I can't do it myself; I'm a success as a therapist, even as I'm a personal failure.

Ideally, an overweight therapist will be emotionally healthy and comfortable enough with her body to reach out and give her client whatever she needs to reach her goals. She may sometimes be a role model, may other times join and commiserate with the client about genetic loading, and still other times use nothing but her clinical skills to help the client examine and resolve her eating difficulties. What is most important is that a therapist recognize that body weight can be a transference and a countertransference issue and use both to keep the client moving forward.

Underweight Therapist and Client

Once again, when both the therapist and client are of low weight or slim—and eating and weight are on the table as therapeutic issues—there are opportunities for automatic bonding but also for false assumptions. Of course, there is slim and then there is undernourished and putting yourself in harm's way; that is, when the therapist is on the slim side of a normal weight range and the client is well below. In this case, the anorexic client might even view the therapist as weighing too much!

When both parties are slender, the undereating client may assume that the therapist hates fatness and overvalues thinness, as the client herself does. She may feel free to rant against fat and comfortable singing the praises of ultraslenderness. If a thin therapist is relatively unbiased about fatness and thinness, she can help her client see that people have value derived from all aspects of personhood, not only appearance. A restrictive eater may also try to bond with a thin therapist by complimenting her on her weight or her clothes, projecting that she would want to hear similar flattery.

Just as it is not unthinkable that an overweight therapist would end up talking about diets with an overweight client, the same thing can happen with a therapist and client who are thin. Although it is tempting to speak about nutrition specific to her own eating, the therapist must be careful to allow her thin client to work through her issues in her own way. Whereas going to a nutritionist may have helped a clinician lose weight and keep it off, doing so may hinder a client from getting in touch with her appetite signals because she may hear what the dietician has to say as yet another food plan.

The therapist may or may not privately overvalue thinness, but she has important work to do in this case to help the client see that a relentless drive toward thinness is dangerous and debilitating. Sadly, the slender therapist may have more credibility than her heavier counterpart in this instance and may be of more help to the client superficially in acknowledging the error of her thinking. She also can use the opportunity to help her client explore what the discussion would be like if she were with a heavier or fat clinician.

If the therapist has not resolved her own eating and weight issues, she may or may not have difficulty helping an undereating, underweight client. If she is going to be of use, she has to know herself inside and out, especially if she fears becoming fat because of cultural taboos or childhood experiences. Her best bet is to use her self-understanding to help the client recognize her terror of putting on weight, which she can do without the discomfort she might have if she were a heavier clinician. The thin therapist can also use her experiences of eating nutritiously and living a healthy lifestyle to show her client that she can keep her weight down in a reasonable, healthful way and not have to resort to starvation, purging, or overexercising.

Therapist Is Overweight and Client Is Underweight

All weight differences between therapists and clients are not the same, that is, it may be more difficult to be a heavy therapist than a slender one when treating eating and weight issues. Whereas the slim therapist probably feels relatively good about her body and can talk openly about fatness and thinness, the heavy therapist may feel ashamed and may not want to put herself out there by bringing up her weight. Interactions can be especially hard (but also highly beneficial) when a therapist is overweight and a client is underweight.

Of course, this is not always the case. Some heavy therapists are quite comfortable in their bodies and exude such self-confidence and competence that clients almost always respond positively to them. They also know how to use the difference in weights between them and the client to help the client grow. They use humor and do not take clients' fat-phobic comments personally. Rather, they allow themselves to be a target in order to help the client understand herself and grow out of her prejudices.

If the therapist is neither so skilled nor so comfortable, a jumble of emotions may fill the therapeutic hour. The thin client, sensing the clinician's unhappiness with or shame about her weight, may not want to hurt or embarrass her and may feel uneasy talking about gaining weight because she imagines the therapist might envy her slimness. Even a client wishing to lose 10 pounds might feel anxious about bringing up this goal, assuming that this is a trivial amount compared to what an obese clinician might want to shed.

A therapist who has struggled unsuccessfully to maintain a healthy weight or who has failed to come to terms with excess pounds may feel that it is petty and superficial for a client to become nearly hysterical because she has put on a pound or two. If the therapist has never been thin and accepts herself as is, she may disdain this culture's rightfully labeled tyranny of slenderness and fail to understand how a client would want to throw all her energy into being a superficial cultural ideal. In truth, a therapist at any weight who does not understand an obsession with thinness may have difficulty empathizing with a client who has an otherwise happy and successful life, but who is terrified to step on the scale and could talk about eating and weight for hours on end.

As was mentioned previously, a thin client who restricts her eating may not believe that a heavy therapist could possibly help her. Based on this assumption, she may avoid bringing up the issue or touch on it only briefly to see if the clinician picks up on it. If, for some reason, the therapist lets the issue pass (even for good clinical reasons), the client may misinterpret the disregard as intentional avoidance. Equally possibly, the therapist might not want to venture into the eating or weight arena because of her own discomfort or because she believes she has nothing to offer her client. In this instance, both parties may be walking on eggshells so that important issues never get raised, never mind resolved.

Therapist Is Underweight and Client Is Overweight

When the therapist is slim or underweight and the client is overweight or obese, the latter might not believe that there is any way she will be understood. She may not consider that the therapist could have once been fatter or very heavy. Particularly if an overweight client is used to being invalidated for his feelings and shamed for his weight, he will have great difficulty bringing up food issues. In this case, most of the initial work should be centered around the therapist making the session safe for the client to talk about his issues, weight and otherwise.

In this case, the therapist's biggest obstacle may be feeling self-conscious about her low weight, and she may avoid bringing up the subject of weight in fear of shaming her client. Her avoidance, however, may make him think she is repulsed by him. Alternately, if she pushes too hard, the clinician runs the risk of making the client so uncomfortable that he retreats (issue and all) into a shell. If she does not give the client enough opportunities to share his discomfort and distress, he may perceive that she is uninterested and unconcerned. This is very tricky work for the clinician, who is trying to create a safe, nonjudgmental environment but also allow the client to pace himself comfortably.

The therapist may not have a clue what it feels like to be overweight or obese and may be afraid of making incorrect assumptions. She may have a negative bias against fat or transference issues from childhood with which to contend. She may feel sorry for her client and helpless to treat him, or she may lack understanding of how he "allowed himself to get so fat." Moreover, she may have the urge to fix him rather than allowing him to resolve his issues in his own way.

Because weight comes off very slowly, if at all, even with the best of efforts, a slim clinician who has never tried to shed pounds or who has had an easy time of it may be very frustrated with her client, especially when he talks about wanting to lose weight in the same breath that he confesses to overeating "all the wrong things." Often, the more helpless she feels about aiding him in weight loss, the more she will push a particular diet program or insist that he exercise. What is really occurring is that her helplessness is mirroring his helplessness around food, which is an excellent entry into talking about the issue.

What happens here is self-defeating for both therapist and client and often leads to treatment that becomes stalled at best and unproductive at worst. The client may unconsciously want the therapist's unconditional acceptance no matter how obese he is and may seduce her into believing that he is there to eat more "normally" and lose weight, when in reality he is testing whether he is lovable as is. The therapist must be aware of this potential scenario and remain neutral, nonjudgmental, and accepting of the client regardless of whether he loses weight. In fact, he may only be able to start when he gives up the quest of being accepted as fat, which often depends on whether the therapist gives up on trying to help him lose weight.

Therapist Is Average Weight and Client Is Over- or Underweight

Although it might seem natural to think that an average-weight therapist would have an easier time with clients at either extreme, this is not necessarily the case. This is because the very nature of the discrepancy between clinician and client body size often gives rise to strong feelings that can then be explored; that is, there is an obvious elephant in the room when the therapist is at one extreme and the client is at another. Whether half-serious jokes are made initially or tentative forays into this difference crop up now and then, the issue usually lives and breathes in the therapy hour and cannot be ignored for long. Painful as it may be for either or both parties, this process generally bodes well for the client who must face his issues, as long as the therapist is skilled and motivated in providing help.

However, when a therapist is of average weight and the client is at either extreme, there is neither the bonding through sameness that can increase trust and attachment or the highly noticeable contrast in body size that can create sufficient tension to drive the topic out into the open. This scenario is not necessarily a problem, but it does make it easier to detour around issues unless therapists or clients are willing to put themselves out there and swing discussion around to eating and weight.

On the other hand, there is much less anxiety for both parties when there are no major weight discrepancies. The therapist of average weight may feel some discomfort raising the issue of a client being fat, but she does not have the baggage of herself being so thin as to make the client uneasy or being so fat that the client may lack faith in her. In effect, her body is not the issue, as it would be if she were thinner or heavier. The client may feel more confidence in an average-weight therapist than a thin one and, therefore, may be more forthcoming with concerns. An underweight client does not have to worry about making an overweight therapist uncomfortable and may feel freer talking about a fear of getting fat and difficulty taking in nourishment.

Therapist Has an Eating, but Not a Weight, Problem and Client Has Either or Both

A therapist who has a hidden eating problem functions along the same lines professionally as one who has substance-abuse difficulties. Of course, these problems run along a continuum from life-threatening anorexia and bulimia to binge eating and controlled restrictive eating (also called lifelong dieting), all common behaviors in our culture. Chronic dieters may not see themselves as having an eating problem because thinness, selectively nutritious eating, and ongoing deprivation in the service of low weight are socially acceptable. Similarly, people who regularly overeat or binge eat may or may not believe that they have a food problem. Some of our perspective on eating is family-based and some is cultural. If a person grows up in a large family and comes from a country in which thinness connotes poverty and ill health, she will not view her eating habits in a negative light.

The point is that, cultural biases aside, some therapists live in denial of having an eating problem when they have one, and cannot validate that clients have one because that would mean facing their own issues. Because their difficulties are hidden by average weight, clients may feed therapists' denial and impede their ability to help with eating and weight issues. Fearful of acknowledging her own difficulties, the therapist may steer discussion away from what makes her uncomfortable. Unaware of her view of thinness or fatness as unrealistic and her restrictive eating or overeating as unhealthy, she may miss that her client has a bona fide eating problem and is undernourished, not fashionably slim, or severely obese, not just chubby.

Because the therapist sees no problem with her (disordered) eating or (unhealthy) weight, the client may be relieved not to have to address her own difficulties and never receive the help she needs and deserves. Clients can be in therapy for a long time without ever addressing eating problems if the therapist does not either fish for or flush them out. This does not mean that clients are not aided with other concerns, even greatly, but that the therapy is limited because of the therapist's inadequacy.

To help raise issues of transference about the therapist's size, ask:

1. Is there anything getting in the way of talking about any of your issues, especially if they relate to eating and weight?

2. Does our difference/sameness in size make it difficult for you to bring up your concerns?

3. Is there anything you want to say that you are holding back for fear of hurting my feelings? For any other reason?

4. How can I help you get more comfortable talking about your weight and eating problems?

There is no magical approach to dealing with issues of eating and weight in therapy, no one-size-fits-all solution. No matter what size issues are involved, some therapists are more naturally direct than others. Others are less confrontational, especially if there is trauma in a client's history, and treat clients as highly fragile (whether they are or not). Sometimes the best we can do is get our clients (and ourselves) ready to face an issue such as being at an unhealthy weight or having eating problems. There may be times when we need a consultation to help us figure out how to broach a subject or help a client relate better to food and their body. We may need supervision to handle strong transference reactions from the client and equally powerful counter-transference feelings of our own. Moreover, we may need to return to therapy ourselves to resolve our issues with food and to keep our bodies healthy and fit.

Reflections for Therapist

1. Now that I understand more about how my eating and weight may affect treating clients with food and body-image issues, how might I react treating thin clients? Fat ones? Chronic dieters? Overeaters? Clients who purge?

2. How can I work with the client's transference? How can I work with my countertransference?

3. What obstacles will I run into working with these
    feelings?
4. Do I need help in the form of a consultation, supervision,
    or therapy to process my countertransference and get
    through my issues?

Here are some guidelines we can follow in dealing with problematic reactions including transference and countertransference.

- We need to err on the side of caution. After bringing up eating or
  weight issues, we must wait and see how the client reacts before
  discussing them further.
- It is important that we make no assumptions about someone's
  appearance (fat, thin or average weight) or their eating as it relates
  to their weight.
- If we sense a client's discomfort about food or weight issues, it is
  crucial to make sure we are not coming across as judgmental.
- If a client regularly avoids talking about food or her body whenever the therapist raises the subject, it is helpful to wonder aloud
  about this reaction and ask for help understanding her reluctance.
- It is important to notice our physical and emotional reactions to a
  client's weight and appearance, to talk about food, especially if we
  feel anxious, contemptuous, disgusted, angry, or envious, and to
  try to understand whether these reactions are due to what the
  client is projecting or our own transference.
- We must avoid trying to "fix" the client's eating or weight problem
  and acknowledge with them feelings of frustration, helplessness,
  and hopelessness.
- Our best bet is to model healthy self-awareness and self-
  acceptance at whatever weight we are without minimizing the difficulties of overcoming eating and weight problems.

If we can do most of these things most of the time, we have a good shot at helping clients resolve their food and body issues. This does not mean that there will not be times when we are highly uncomfortable or cause enormous discomfort to clients. It is our job to cause pain in the short run to alleviate it in the long run. The more we consider issues of eating and weight and how they may play out in the therapeutic relationship, the better we will be at addressing them with confidence and competence.

CHAPTER 11

Treatment
Options

Although there is no right way to address eating and weight issues, there are a number of avenues in which the subject may come up naturally and appropriately. Our goal is not to force the issue but to find moments in the therapy when these subjects arise organically. This chapter will illustrate ways that the topic may surface and be treated without it being a stretch for either therapist or client.

The more attuned you are to the possibility of clients having difficulties with food or their weight, the better you will be at creating space for this discussion as therapy rolls along. Here are some tried-and-true ways to raise these issues.

As a Health/Medical Issue

The most obvious approach is through concerns about medical risks, quality of life, or how to stay healthy. This avenue can be productive as long as we avoid lecturing clients about the dangers of being over- or underweight. The best way to find out what they know about the health risks of being obese or severely underweight is to ask them. You can provide clients with a handout of medical risks, refer them to legitimate Web sites, and give them a bibliography of books and articles. Most clients welcome information. Not only do they appreciate being educated, but education helps them feel nurtured and valued.

Sometimes a client will know more about the subject of health than we do. But what they *know* is only half the picture; the rest is what they *do* with this knowledge, and that is where we pick up the ball. If a client possesses a wealth of information about exercise and nutrition but cannot seem to apply it to herself, this paradox is fodder for interesting clinical discussion, as is talking with a client who disparages research studies and is prone to rely on anecdotal information alone or ignores even that.

It is useful to obtain a release of information to talk with a client's health practitioners, especially her primary care doctor. Although some may not talk with us, doctors may be relieved to know that they are not alone in caring for a patient with weight issues and that someone is handling the psychological aspect of patient care. One of the problems in talking with doctors (or nutritionists) is that the majority will insist that the client go on a diet or join a weight-loss program. This is true no matter how much weight the client has to lose or how many times they have dieted and regained pounds. Every therapist has to decide for herself whether she believes that diets will work for a client and proceed accordingly. In general, if we can assure doctors that we are working on helping clients eat more healthily and lose weight *in the long run*, they will forgo turning up the heat on diets. The goal is for all treaters to be on the same page.

We need to be aware of the possibility for triangulation, as it is easy to get stuck in the middle of a tug-of-war between client and practitioner. Our best bet is to help the client assess pros and cons at every decision point so she can make up her mind about how to proceed, then be as supportive as possible. Although clients know my bias against diet programs, many find the structure of Weight Watchers useful, and I do not object to their attending meetings or following their rules. Although we want to exhibit clear values, we also want to model flexible behavior that is in our clients' best interest.

Occasionally, we might encounter a client who is considering bariatric surgery. If we know nothing about the subject, we need to say so. Usually a client is willing to share information she has been given, but it is not enough to rely on her take on these procedures. It helps to have a working knowledge of benefits and risks to assist a client in deciding whether to proceed, especially regarding postsurgery motivation to eat differently. Many clients who seek bariatric surgery have tried other pounds-off plans and programs and failed; they view surgery as a life-saving last resort. Other clients are engaging in magical thinking and want to avoid the work of planning meals, controlling eating impulses and portion size, and changing their relationship with food.

To help the client view food and weight issues from a health perspective, ask:

1. How much of a health risk are your weight and eating habits?
2. Have you discussed your eating and weight with a doctor? If not, why not?
3. What are the medical recommendations you have received and have you followed them? If not, why not?
4. How can I help you improve your health by changing your eating?

As a Self-care/Self-esteem Issue

If we intend to address eating or weight concerns as part of low self-esteem and poor self-care, we need to be certain that, in fact, one is related to the other by making sure that the client does not have an underlying medical or medication issue that is causing problems. By exploring the subject gently, we can find out how the client views her self-caretaking and perceives her self-esteem. Many clients will say right off that they have low self-esteem and connect it to having weight problems.

Because the term *self-esteem* is bandied about these days, we need a solid working definition. Nathaniel Branden, author of *The Six Pillars of Self-Esteem*, states: "Self-esteem has two interrelated components. One is a sense of basic confidence in the face of life's challenges: *self-efficacy.* The other is a sense of being worthy of happiness: *self-respect*" (1994, p. 26). If we plan to talk with clients about how their eating and weight issues might be a reflection of low self-esteem, we need to examine their ability to empower themselves as well as their sense of deservedness. Using Branden's definition, we can move beyond a client saying she does not feel good about herself and must have low self-esteem to a joint exploration of why she might lack confidence, not be up to the challenge of eating in a healthy, pleasurable manner, feel undeserving of happiness, and lack self-respect and self-worth.

Approaching the subject through a self-care lens, we can begin discussion by asking the client to rate her self-care ability on a scale of 1 to 10 (1 being *poor care* and 10 being *excellent care*). But we must be careful: It is easy to view an overweight or bulimic client as not taking care of herself well, yet see one who eats only health foods and spends hours at the gym as someone who does. A good rule of thumb is to look for behavior that is rigid, compulsive, and extreme—overeating or excessive caloric restriction, being a total couch potato or never missing a workout, refusing to get on a scale, or obsessing about gaining a pound over a certain arbitrary number.

When talking to clients about self-care, include these four realms: physical, emotional, mental, and spiritual. Physical self-care includes going to the doctor when sick, taking preventive measures to protect health, not ignoring, denying or minimizing medical problems, and following doctors' advice when appropriate. Emotional self-care involves tolerating painful emotions, regulating affect effectively, setting and keeping healthy boundaries, and not using destructive behaviors to manage feelings. Mental self-care consists of staying sharp, challenging the mind, engaging in ongoing learning, being creative, and remaining aware of world happenings. Spiritual self-care includes finding meaning in life, coming to terms with loss and death, and feeling connected to the earth, its people, and future generations.

It is wise to tread lightly in talking with clients about self-care, because if we dig deeply enough (or with some clients, barely scratch the surface), we are likely to uncover shame. Many clients are caught in a distressing paradox of knowing how to take care of themselves and not doing it. In fact, sometimes the more they are aware of what they *should* do, the less inclined they are to do it. They therefore end up feeling shame about their eating or size along with their unwillingness, failure, or inability to do anything about it. Some clients will be so uncomfortable when they experience shame about poor self-care that they will shift into denial or minimization, while others will exhibit despair. The wise clinician will gently explore shame and how it gets played out in relation to food and body.

When discussing self-care, it is important not to take an all-or-nothing view of a client's caretaking ability. Clients may take outstanding care of themselves in some areas and mediocre or poor care in others. An overweight client may have regular medical checkups and age-appropriate tests, work out consistently, and not eat junk food. Her "self-care" downfall may be failing to control portion size or engaging in emotional eating. A bulimic client might eat nutritiously most of the time and only purge when she eats "bad" foods.

One of the most productive discussions with a client is how she uses food as a reward; that is, taking care of herself by giving herself a food treat. After all, we are surrounded by media messages that say good self-care involves gratifying ourselves with external things, including food. Parents often use treats as an incentive for and reinforcement of acceptable behavior and there was even a time when a child received a lollipop for "being good" when he went to the doctor!

When clients use food as a primary reward, they are limited in effective ways of providing self-care. We can explain that "normal" eaters use food occasionally as a treat or pick-me-up, but that food should not be the primary means of self-reward. The heart of the matter is that treats are not really a reward or good for us; when eaten on a regular basis, they clog our arteries and fill our bloodstream with toxic chemicals. The problem is that food *feels* like a reward because it is culturally promoted as one and registers in our brain's pleasure center. This does not mean it is a healthy choice.

Clients who use food as a primary reward can learn to take care of themselves more effectively. It helps to explain that every time they use food inappropriately, they are missing out on a more appropriate response—calling friends when they receive a promotion rather than celebrating alone by eating half an apple pie, putting on music and dancing their heart out after a stressful day with the kids, or losing themselves between the pages of a book when, finally, Friday arrives.

Helping clients find better ways to reward themselves starts with changing beliefs. Most clients who abuse food think or say to themselves, "I deserve this treat." They believe that—pardon the pun—food is their just dessert, and need to understand that, yes, they *deserve* the treat (and everything else good in life), but that deservedness is not the issue. The crux of the matter is not what they deserve, but what is a beneficial choice. As soon as a client insists that she deserves something, I know that something is fishy in her self-esteem/self-care department. People who believe they are deserving do not need to prove it; it is a given, like the earth, moon, and stars.

Of course, it is easy to see how clients can become confused about food usage based on the incentives and reinforcements they experienced in childhood and our culture's relentless emphasis on external (usually material), rather than internal, reward. It is our job to explore and, if necessary, correct client misconceptions about deservedness by educating them about how to make healthy choices they can be proud of, which, in turn, will expand their self-care options and raise their self-esteem.

To help the client assess if food and weight problems are related to poor self-care and/or low-self esteem, ask:

1. How good are you at taking care of yourself—physically, emotionally, mentally, and spiritually?
2. Do you have an effective repertoire of emotional self-care skills? What are they?
3. If you are poor at self-care, why do you think that is and what can you do about it?
4. How would you rate your self-esteem (excellent, good, fair, poor)?
5. Which of your attitudes or behaviors contribute to low self-esteem?
6. What ways could you change your thinking to improve your self-esteem?
7. What actions could you take to improve your self-esteem?

As a Self-soothing/Comfort Issue

It is hardly surprising that many people use food to soothe themselves when they are in emotional distress. For the biological reasons described earlier, as well as from early socialization, it is natural to turn to food for comfort. Carbohydrates do help us calm down and zone out. The bliss of being held and fed is a memory connection of which we might not be conscious, but nevertheless exists deep in our psyche. On the other hand, most of us probably remember getting treats as a child when we were feeling down or upset. Eating for comfort is made easy because food is both accessible and delicious.

Although some people completely lose their appetite when they come down with the blahs or the blues, most are likely to at least occasionally incline toward food. Clients who regularly eat to avoid or minimize experiencing uncomfortable or painful emotions must be helped on two fronts: learning to turn to people rather than food when they are upset, and developing emotional resources to bear pain on their own. Although most clients understand that choosing food as their primary comfort is self-destructive behavior, many are terrified of giving it up and literally know no other way of making themselves feel better. This same destructive mindset is true for undereaters who obsess about food and weight to ward off or distract from intense feelings.

One way to steer clients toward health is to help them see that other people will be there for them when they are troubled—starting, of course, with us. Developing trust involves changing cognitions about trusting and depending on people, and a willingness to take psychological risks and share distress. By reaching out, clients learn that, indeed, many folks are happy and willing to listen to and support them and that when they are not, for the most part, clients can bear their hurt and upset alone. By developing internal and external sources of comfort and containment, clients can reduce food-seeking behaviors.

In a similar vein, many clients eat or obsess about food and recipes to fill an inner emptiness. Disconnected from their internal selves and from others, food is the be-all and end-all of their existence. As long as they can fill up on food or good feelings about being thin, they feel fine. Although they may be hungry for love, affection, connection, companionship, meaning, passion, and joy—things that are truly nourishing to the heart and soul—these desires pose too many risks on which to take a chance.

Our work with clients who soothe inner emptiness by abusing food is to help them recognize that only by going deeply into their emptiness will they be able to learn what will truly fill them up. We need to help them identify what exactly they yearn for. This is a lengthy process. Clients need a great deal of support in taking small steps that will lead them away from abusing food to discovering what nourishes them. A word of caution: We must be wary of feeding clients too much too soon and trying to fill them up too quickly. We must try to be patient and help them tolerate inner or existential emptiness and angst long enough for it to lead them to what they can do to create a more fulfilling life.

To help the client assess if food problems are related to an inability to comfort and soothe themselves without abusing food, ask:

1. What are effective ways you comfort yourself when you're in emotional pain?
2. If you abuse food (obsessing about and avoiding/overeating) when you're upset, how does it help soothe and comfort you?
3. What else have you tried to get relief from emotional distress?
4. What are you willing to try to overcome your eating problems?
5. How might therapy help you become more effective in handling distressing emotions?

As a Stress Reduction Issue

Clients often talk about being stressed when they mean they are feeling overwhelmed, impatient, frustrated, angry, pressured, stuck, undervalued, or overworked. They believe that people are making too many demands on them that they fear they cannot meet. Sometimes they stress themselves out by being perfectionists who are unable to prioritize, finish tasks, or delegate effectively. Whatever stress means to them, it frequently drives them to eat or obsess about food.

Unlike feelings such as hurt and disappointment, stress hijacks not merely our hearts but our bodies—clients feel fatigued or agitated, or they develop intestinal or back problems, headaches, or other ailments. Therefore, when we address food abuse due to stress, we must engage clients in treatment on two levels: reducing physical symptoms and helping them identify and diffuse the emotions that produce them.

Primarily, we need to teach stressed clients how to relax without food. Kicking back might come from watching TV, reading, playing with the dog, taking a walk or a bath, calling a friend, practicing yoga, napping, or listening to music. Some clients feel better becoming physically active; others need to be still and chill. They often need immediate strategies that are easy to implement, such as deep breathing, using a mantra, or writing in a journal. Gradually we can introduce the idea of hobbies and practices such as yoga and exercise so they can keep themselves on a more even keel and prevent stress.

We also must encourage clients to identify the causes of stress, especially whether it is primarily internal or external. The goal is for them to recognize what emotions underlie "stress" and whether they can do something about them. Generally we are talking about helplessness, confusion, frustration, and feeing overwhelmed. If a client is always anxious about being on time or performing perfectly, he will need to change his beliefs in order to reduce anxiety, that is, to be more accepting of lateness and imperfection. Alternately, if he has an abusive or highly critical boss or wife, or a demanding friend or parent, he will need to alter his situation to reduce stress. Often clients need to work on reacting differently to trying situations at the same time as they change them.

To help the client assess his stress level, its cause, and its connection to disordered eating, ask:

1. What is your general stress level (high, medium, low)?
2. What situations cause you the most stress?
3. What emotions do you feel when you are stressed?
4. Would any of the following help you not abuse food: stop trying to be perfect or "do it all," say no more often, lower your standards for other people, accept mistakes and failure, show more compassion to yourself?
5. Are there situations that would be less stressful if you made changes in your attitude or behavior?
6. Are there stressful situations that need to be changed because they are harmful to your health and well-being?
7. What can you do to modulate stress other than abuse food?
8. How can I help you learn to cope with stress more effectively?

As an Interpersonal/Intimacy Issue

Sometimes an eating and weight problem is like a football thrown back and forth between people—mothers and daughters, spouses, even siblings or friends. The problem becomes triangulated into the diad, takes on a life of its own, and serves the unit in an unhealthy way. When food and weight become a constant or chronic source of argument within a couple, precluding or diluting emotional intimacy, the problem moves from being merely intrapsychic to interpersonal.

For example, overeating and being overweight may unconsciously be the only way a daughter can show her thin-obsessed, controlling mother that she is her own person. Being nagged about getting fat may be the way a wife receives attention from her distant husband; remaining on a constant diet and insisting on healthy meals made from scratch may be the way a husband feels special and taken care of by his busy wife. Maybe a partner remains fat because if she grows thin she will feel attractive enough to act on her unhappiness and go out and find another mate. Maybe a spouse becomes a compulsive exerciser to avoid his partner's company and the reluctant admission that there has been no intimacy between them for decades. Or perhaps having an eating problem is an attempt to ask for unconditional love, warts and all.

When we sense that food, weight, or body problems indicate that something has gone awry in a relationship, we can frame them as couples issues and address them individually or suggest couples therapy. This same approach holds true with a mother and daughter or any other diad in which food and weight are symptomatic of dysfunctional dynamics. Nowhere is the pitched battle about weight more pronounced than in children trying to separate from parents. Generally females act out in the food and weight arena more often than males, but the dynamics are the same for either gender. Commonly (but not always) Mother is controlling about food and other issues and Father is somewhere in the background. Sometimes Mother is thin and tries to do everything in her power to make her child follow suit. Or Mother may be overweight herself and may micromanage her child's eating so that she will not become fat.

More often than not, double messages and double binds abound and family dysfunction goes deep. It is possible that the client's parents are having (and always have had) intimacy difficulties and that the client's eating problems are getting triangulated into their interpersonal struggles. Family therapy can be highly useful to free up the adult child to separate and gain autonomy—and to learn to eat "normally." Even if the family does not agree to come in, using a family systems perspective can be enormously helpful in individual treatment.

To help the client recognize that eating and weight problems may have an interpersonal aspect, ask:

1. Who are the people in your life who care about and/or comment on your eating and/or weight?
2. What do they say and how do you feel about it?
3. Is your eating or body size meant to give them any kind of message? If so, how could you give them this message in a healthier, more effective way?
4. Do you ever give responsibility for your eating over to an intimate (for example, asking your spouse or a friend to prevent you from eating certain foods)? Do you ever blame people for "making you have food or weight problems" (for example, saying that if your mother didn't upset you, you wouldn't eat)?
5. Are there ways that your food problems get played out between you and others?
6. How can I help you make changes in your relationships so that you will have a healthier connection to food and other people?

As a Metaphor for Other Problems

Sometimes we need to address eating and weight problems as symbols of other issues. For example, a client who was neglected in childhood and feels insignificant, weak, and powerless might (unconsciously or consciously) imagine that his large size provides him with power and substance. He may fear becoming thin because he equates slenderness with being invisible and ineffective. The work of the therapist includes helping the client recognize that power comes from within and that he can be at a lower, healthier weight and still be assertive and strong.

Clients who have difficulty talking about or letting go of a traumatic past may use eating problems as a way to show the world that they have suffered. Being under- or oversized distinguishes them from other people whom they often perceive as normal and problem-free. Our goal is to help them explore and share their past appropriately so that they do not have to wear their weight as an emblem of suffering, and to change their view of themselves from victim to survivor.

There are clients who use weight and food problems as a way to get other people to take care of them. Often they have endured severe emotional abandonment or had nonnurturing parents who competed with their needs. Through an ongoing eating or weight problem, the client continues to engage the parent (or, in displacement, a partner, friends, colleagues, or the therapist) and assures himself that he will not be emotionally abandoned. In this case, we need to encourage the client to strengthen his inner resources to take care of himself and also teach him how to relate to people on a more independent, mature level.

Some clients are stuck in the dilemma of feeling a need to struggle to be happy versus leading a contented, satisfying life. Perhaps their parental role models were unfulfilled or would not allow themselves to sit back and enjoy accomplishments. Maybe the family believed that happiness equaled smugness or arrogance or that, once achieved, happiness would not last. Or perhaps the client was taught that a person must always work hard and never rest or slack off. These clients equate being a "normal" eater and maintaining a comfortable, healthy weight with being perfect and self-satisfied. Treatment allows them to reframe irrational beliefs and develop a rational cognitive system that supports achievement and contentment and allows them to feel good (not bad) about being functional around food.

To help the client identify ways that food abuse and weight concerns may be a metaphor for other needs, ask:

1. What might your food or weight problems say to people that you have difficulty saying more directly?
2. How could you express yourself more appropriately?
3. Could we continue to explore whether food issues might be a metaphor for underlying wants and needs that you are having difficulty expressing?

Just as there is no single best approach to treating substance abuse, depression, low self-esteem, or borderline personality, there is no one way to deal with eating and weight issues. Some complaints will be so easy to remedy that we are able to talk through them and steer a client in the right direction in one or two sessions—a postmenopausal woman might feel relief to learn that weight gain is common at this time of life and accept that she might put on a few pounds; a frail elder who can no longer get out to grocery-shop might be grateful for getting help signing up for Meals on Wheels; a college freshman who has dropped a few pounds might be reassured that decreased interest in food is not unusual in transitional and/or stressful times and that he will probably regain his normal appetite when he has settled in.

Other concerns will take more time and discussion but, remember, even clinicians specializing in eating disorders do not talk about food and weight every minute of each session. Eating might be at the core of discussion, but dialogue shoots off in various directions: self-care, neurotransmitters, marital problems, or early trauma. Often over- or undereating is a symptom of deeper problems due to a general lack of impulse control or a serious medical condition. Other times food dysfunction will be connected less to biology and the family tree than to unhealthy current habits or to relationship difficulties that are being played out in the food arena.

A client who comes to therapy with an eating problem may be disappointed, shocked, or angry that his difficulties are about more than food. He may be "resistant" to talking about anything else and insist that sessions focus on his food abuse in order to get "cured" fast. We might need to go along with targeting food, until other issues crowd the picture or we find a golden opportunity to suggest that specific issues might be impacting his eating. Other clients may talk about everything under the sun even though they insist they are miserable about their weight and we must bide our time until they are ready to face the music. Sometimes the best we can do is negotiate if it is all right for us to raise the subject if they do not.

As a cognitive-behavioral therapist who works off the assumption that beliefs generate feelings and behaviors, I naturally use this treatment approach most often. This model makes sense to me and appears to make sense to clients as well. Although I do not explicitly talk about beliefs, behaviors, and emotions at each session, this therapeutic change model is the underpinning of all my questions and comments, and generally clients adapt this approach to other concerns by focusing on how their thinking affects their behavior and experiences with emotions.

As time goes on, however, I have realized that talk therapy will take clients just so far because our eating is connected to so many unconscious events and memories. Basically I will use any treatment model that will not cause harm and has the potential to help. Some approaches appear to advance the therapy overnight, while others may be a bust and go nowhere. Moreover, some clients are motivated good sports who will try just about anything to resolve eating issues. They follow recommendations and usually benefit from being open-minded and goal-oriented. Other clients adamantly refuse (for good and not so good reasons) to try something different, and pushing them only bogs down sessions in struggle.

There are two types of medication to be considered for people with eating problems, whether these are ongoing or situational: those that aid weight loss or weight gain and those that work on rebalancing neurotransmitters and treat depressive, bipolar, and anxiety disorders. It makes sense that clients who are less depressed and anxious will have more effective self-care, will be more motivated to exercise and eat right, and have improved impulse control and higher energy levels. Many clients with eating problems report an increased ability to curb disordered eating when taking medications for anxiety and depression. Whether this is due to drugs remedying underlying chemical imbalances or acting directly on appetite is unclear.

Most of us have had experiences with clients who are eager to try medications and others who will close the door on discussion the moment we bring it up. Sometimes clients will ask us if they should take particular medications, and sometimes we raise the question. My bias is toward medications that mitigate underlying conditions such as depression and anxiety, and against weight-loss drugs except in the most extreme cases. It pays to be cautious when clients want to know about weight-loss drugs, whether over the counter or prescribed. They are a great temptation to disordered eaters, some of whom are looking for a quick fix and some of whom have been struggling with weight for decades and are looking for anything that will help.

Many weight-loss drugs are not FDA-approved and are downright dangerous. We need to take a step back from the client's desire to lose weight to make sure she is not harming herself by using supplements, herbs, or drugs. We may even need to voice a strong opinion on the subject rather than remain clinically neutral. Certainly, we want to document any discussion about these medications in our therapy notes.

Most experts agree that weight-loss medications should be used only by clients who are at serious medical risk due to excess weight and not for "cosmetic purposes." "Prescription weight-loss drugs are approved only for those with a body mass index (BMI) of 30 and above, or 27 and above if they have obesity-related conditions, such as high blood pressure, dyslipidemia (abnormal amounts of fat in the blood), or type 2 diabetes" ("Prescription Medications for the Treatment of Obesity," U.S. Department of Health and Human Services Web site). Of course, this is not the message promoted by pharmaceutical companies, so we must always steer clients in the direction of bona fide clinical (replicable, double-blind) studies and reliable sources to determine a drug's efficacy. Although the World Wide Web is a wonderful resource, it is no substitute for rigorous scientific study and sound medical advice.

There are different kinds of weight-loss drugs. Appetite suppressants decrease appetite and increase the sensation of fullness. FDA-approved phentermine and sibutramine are the most commonly prescribed appetite suppressants in the United States. Then there are the FDA-approved lipase inhibitors Meridia and Xenical, which reduce the body's ability to absorb fat. A popular, over-the-counter lipase inhibitor is the drug Alli (a.k.a. generic orlistat). "Off label" drugs (which are FDA-approved for one condition and used to treat another) are also used to promote weight loss. Antidepressants have been known to aid weight loss, but most only work for a short period of time. "Although certain psychiatric medications can cause weight gain in the general population, none has had this effect with malnourished anorexic patients. Recent exciting studies suggest that olanzapine (Zyprexa) and other medications in this class may finally offer a drug that can help some low-weight anorexia nervosa patients. Olanzapine lessens anxiety and obsessional thinking, and some anorexic patients find they feel less paralyzed due to rigid thinking and behavior on this medication" (Mickley, 2004, p.1). The only FDA-approved medication for bulimia is fluoxetine, which in studies appears to have a success rate similar to cognitive-behavioral therapy.

In addition to medication, there are other approaches that may enhance clients' relationship with food and their bodies. Here are some useful treatment models:

Cognitive-behavioral therapy (CBT) is based on the principle that our beliefs create our feelings and behaviors—change your thinking and your emotions and behaviors follow suit. Most mental health studies find CBT highly successful in treating any number of conditions, including eating disorders. CBT can be done within the primary therapy (it is not difficult to learn) or a client can be referred to an expert to work on specific irrational thoughts regarding food, eating, weight, and body.

CBT works well for clients who do not wish to "dredge up the past" or "dwell" on painful feelings, and folks who have limited time (or money) for therapy and want to keep a strict focus on the here and now. CBT gets right to the root of victim think. Clients are generally amazed at how irrational thinking dictates obsessional and dysfunctional behavior around food and can apply reframing beliefs to bettering many parts of their lives. With practice, most clients can use the process on their own, but it can be difficult for clients with limited ability to stay focused because of being overwhelmed with feelings (or for other reasons). Paradoxically, it is the shift from emotion to cognition that helps these clients contain overwhelming feelings.

Internal family systems (IFS) is a combination of a systems framework and positive reframing based on the theory that we each have internal parts of our psyche doing their best to care for us. Toward this end, different aspects of ourselves (called the self, exiles, managers, firefighters) arise to do different jobs. IFS does not aim to eliminate these parts, including the ones that drive disordered eating, but to acknowledge each one and integrate them all.

For clients who are filled with shame about their weight or food abuse, it is easy to see how IFS would be beneficial. Rather than thinking about giving up binge eating or bulimia, clients can view the behavior as trying to help them cope and protect their more fragile self-parts. Behavior is seen as purposeful but misguided, not as bad. IFS is user friendly, but clinicians should employ it cautiously with clients who have or may have dissociative disorders. This population might find IFS confusing if they are doing other therapeutic work to eliminate or integrate "subselves."

Eye movement desensitization reprocessing (EMDR), an integrative therapy, is an excellent way of unlocking and detoxifying memories for disordered eaters who have endured childhood or adult trauma. Through use of bilateral (sound, eye movement, or tactile) stimulation while focusing on a traumatic memory or a current emotional distress, the client experiences strong abreactions that are then reprocessed appropriately.

It is unclear exactly how EMDR changes the brain. Over the last two decades many valid studies have confirmed its success, but it remains controversial. Three out of the four clients whom I referred to seasoned EMDR professionals had success in moving past large and small traumas (the fourth client had difficulty making any progress in long-term treatment). This approach works best when the client has a functioning ego structure and is willing to explore emotional pain, past or present. A good deal of discussion about EMDR should occur before the client engages in it.

Dialectical behavioral training (DBT) is a psychosocial treatment designed for clients with BPD (which correlates strongly with eating disorders), a combination of behaviorism, cognitive therapy, and mindfulness. It is most commonly used in a combination of individual and group work treatment focused on decreasing self-harming behaviors and expanding life skills such as core mindfulness, emotion regulation, interpersonal effectiveness, and distress tolerance.

DBT is especially helpful in changing thinking, curbing impulsive behavior, and teaching effective emotional management. It is highly useful for clients who have difficulty managing impulses and distressing emotions, but it is usually a long-term commitment that may take anywhere from several weeks to a year.

Gestalt therapy has a focus on (what is perceived and experienced as) the here and now, on taking responsibility for self, and on one's relationship to environment. Because it grounds them in their senses, this approach is useful for clients who are stuck in the past or regularly project themselves into the future. For a client who is disconnected from her body, it is a simple approach to help reground her. Clients also learn to view themselves as consisting of parts that make up a whole so that instead of seeing only their weight or disordered eating, they can envision themselves more completely and learn to value their entire self.

Several techniques of Gestalt therapy are helpful in the eating and weight arenas, including the empty chair, role-playing, and letter writing. Many clients enjoy role-playing and letter writing because they find the experiences freeing. However, role-playing can also make clients uncomfortable and they may refuse to do it. It is wise to revisit the issue every once in a while to see if the client can make better use of the technique as therapy progresses because it is such a helpful tool in getting disordered thinking and behavior around food to speak for itself.

Psychodrama is a powerful approach that is part theater and part group therapy and uses experiential methods to explore thinking and behaving. A group leader assists the client in using group members to help her act or play out troubling interactions and situations. The experience is then thoroughly processed under the direction of the group leader. One of the most powerful aspects of this approach is that clients bring their pain out of hiding and, through the witnessing of group members, receive the validation and feedback that is needed to unstick them from unhealthy patterns.

Some clients take to psychodrama like ducks to water, but most are somewhat frightened of it at first. It is not recommended for clients who are too shy or lack the ego strength to function well in a group, as it deals with very powerful emotions in a public setting. Clients who are risk takers and enjoy group interaction and feedback usually value and benefit from the experience.

Couples therapy is helpful to clients with eating and weight issues that are embedded in dysfunctional diad dynamics. Because our earliest feedings involve connection to another person, eating has major interpersonal influences. Eating may be done in isolation, but it is never a purely intrapsychic experience; even the most secret gorging involves thoughts of and reactions to other people (past and present). What a client weighs is also not merely a personal concern, but one that affects her ability to be social and sexual and to relate to others.

Sometimes a client is willing to have her partner join her in session but, as often as not, she will refuse. It is worthwhile revisiting the issue if the therapy gets stuck, especially if the client is unable to make significant progress in changing her eating patterns. Because couples therapy can be frightening, clients sometimes have to see that there is no other way to help themselves, that is, that they cannot recover from their food problems without resolving their couples issues.

Family therapy is a powerful approach to treating eating problems. Whenever possible, even if we are not comfortable actually "doing" family therapy, we should invite family members in to become acquainted, form an alliance, gather information, and be educated about their family member's eating problems. Clients may take a bit of coaching and encouragement to agree to family therapy, but in the hands of a skilled clinician, amazing progress can be made as all the parties start to understand that the identified patient's problems are not wholly about food and weight, but about much larger and deeper issues, and that everyone plays a role in them.

Family work is most beneficial for clients whose family relationships are substantially dysfunctional. Sometimes the client is doing his best to change, but the forces against him are simply too powerful and intervention is needed. As with couples therapy, the client may have to reach an impasse with eating problems before agreeing to family therapy.

Group therapy is an excellent mode for disordered eaters who have serious relational problems and sufficient ego strength to help them overcome shame. It helps them become more accepting of themselves and teaches them to reach out and rely on others. It is especially helpful in showing clients that their basic problem is not with food but with people.

Not every client is a good candidate for group therapy. It may be contraindicated for those who have major trust issues that preclude them from taking feedback well and for clients who lack sufficient impulse control to function appropriately in a group. On the other hand, most clients will benefit enormously from group therapy.

The majority of clients with eating and weight problems profit from being in any kind of nondiet group that encourages emotional and interpersonal growth.

- *Self-esteem groups* can do wonders for clients who have difficulty seeing themselves as deserving of being healthy and attractive. Women especially benefit from being in a safe setting where they can learn to share feelings, take risks, set boundaries, speak up, and take care of their own needs.

- *Assertiveness training* teaches essential life skills that clients, especially females, need to set limits, confront others, stand up for themselves, and learn to express anger appropriately in order to not abuse food.

- *Eating support groups* (for general eating problems or for anorexia, bulimia, or binge eating disorders specifically) provide a nonjudgmental, nonconfrontational setting that focuses on individual thinking and behavior and not on group process. These groups are helpful for clients who are too fragile for group therapy or are only motivated to work on eating (and not other) problems.

- *Psychoeducational workshops* (such as my "Quit Fighting with Food" workshop) offer a structured environment to acquire new skills and practice new food-related behaviors. Clients who find group work too "touchy feely" or emotionally threatening will often take a workshop that is skills-based, time-limited, and educationally focused.

- *Parenting groups* teach moms and dads new ways to cope so that they can give up abusing food and give them ideas on how to feed their children to promote "normal" eating. Clients who will not join a group focusing on their own eating will often attend one to help their children eat healthily.

- *Caretaking groups* are helpful because a substantial number of people who overeat are either major caretakers or have overly nurturing personalities. These groups are a back door into teaching them to care for themselves without food.

- *A men's or women's group* is a safe place to explore and discuss gender-related concerns that affect eating and weight, including sexuality and intimacy. These groups work well for eating-disordered clients who have been sexually abused and are uncomfortable with the opposite sex.

- *Groups for depression, anxiety, or obsessive-compulsive disorder (OCD)* afford an opportunity for clients to learn how these clinical disorders affect their eating and weight. They work well for clients who think of themselves as primarily depressed or anxious rather than eating disordered.

There is no end to the tools available, within and outside therapy, to help clients with eating or weight problems. *Journaling* is useful for some, but stressful for those who have difficulty expressing feelings in writing. Journals can target activities, feelings, or beliefs and may be general or have an eating and weight-related focus. Journaling is also a useful way for clients to recognize unhealthy patterns, such as food shopping when they are tired, and chart their progress, especially when they minimize successes. Alternately, if they have artistic talent, clients can draw or paint their emotional moods.

Body work such as massage, meditation, yoga, tai chi, and dance, among others, can help clients with food problems connect to their physical selves. The goal is to help them feel more comfortable in and about their body. Any activity, in fact, can increase body awareness— boxing, kung fu, skating, fencing, horseback riding, swimming, skiing, or bicycling—as long as the client stays focused on movement as opposed to rote actions or competition.

Massage helps most clients relax and feel connected to their body, but it can also bring up painful feelings about past trauma, especially of a sexual nature. *Visualization* works for many clients, yet may actually increase anxiety in those who are already highly anxious. The same holds true for *meditation.* Anxious clients often do better relaxing through keeping their bodies moving to discharge nervous energy than by sitting still. One technique that any client can use and benefit from is *deep breathing*. It is useful not only for relaxation but to prevent food abuse. Because it travels well, clients can do it just about anywhere.

Other learning and support tools can be found on the Internet in the form of *Web sites, blogs, and message boards.* In addition to national Web sites that deal with anorexia, bulimia and binge eating disorder, there are smaller ones that focus on giving up dieting, eating normally, learning how to cope with stress and distress without abusing food, and creating a healthy, positive body image at any size. My rule of thumb is to check out a site before referring a client to it.

Blogs are online essays on just about anything, including food, weight, and body image. Bite-sized pieces of learning, they work well with clients who are too busy or unfocused to read a book, take a class, or join a group. *Message boards* are Internet sites on which people post ideas and thoughts on a specific topic, anonymously or with self-identifiers. (The sites I advise on are run by a qualified moderator and promote nondieting and normal eating.) They are helpful for clients fearful of groups or who are isolated because of health, geography, or temperament.

One final way to move clients along the road to recovery from eating and weight problems is to recognize when the therapy is not giving them the help they need. Good therapy means knowing what we know and what we do not know. Getting a *consultation* on a difficult case is often highly useful in learning what therapeutic direction to take or discovering how to get sessions unstuck. Sometimes a consultation from an eating disorders specialist provides new insights and innovative approaches.

If a consultation does not help, clinicians should not be afraid to make a *referral* to an eating disorders expert. I sometimes work with a client for one or a few sessions to see if my assessment of the situation can add anything to what the primary therapist is doing. Usually, based on decades of experience, I can spot patterns or themes that have been unseen, ignored, minimized, or remain hidden. Sometimes I do nothing more than repeat what the therapist has already told the client, but because I am new and considered an "expert," the client may take my words more seriously.

The field of food issues is constantly changing as new theories on appetite and weight loss emerge and new medications and medical procedures prove helpful. The best we can do is try to keep abreast, stay present to our clients' concerns, and hone our skills. Hopefully, this book has demystified the subject of treating food and weight issues as they emerge in the therapeutic hour by providing enough information so that every clinician feels more confident and competent in exploring this most challenging subject.

References

American Academy of Family Physicians. (n.d.). Retrieved January 11, 2008, from http://www.familydoctor.org.

American Heart Association. (n.d.). Retrieved January 11, 2008, from http://www.americanheart.org.

American Psychiatric Association. (1994). *Diagnostic and statistical manual of mental disorders IV-R* (M. B. First, Ed.). Washington, DC: Author.

Anorexia Nervosa and Related Eating Disorders. (n.d.). Retrieved January 12, 2008, from http://www.anred.com.

Blumenthal, D. (2007, October 6). Beauty: Being underweight can weigh heavily. *The New York Times* online. Retrieved January 11, 2008, from http://query.nytimes.com/gst/fullpage.html?sec=health&st=cse&sq=Being+underweight+can+weigh+heavily&scp=1.

Branden, N. (1994). *The Six Pillars of Self-Esteem*. New York: Bantam.

Brodey, J. (2005, September 20). Blacks join the eating-disorder mainstream. *The New York Times* online. Retrieved January 11, 2008, from http://www.nytimes.com/2005/09/20/health/psychology/20eat.html?st=cse&sq=Blacks+join+the+eating-disorder+mainstream&scp=1.

Buchwald, H., Avidor, Y., Braunwald, E., Jensen, M. D., Pories, W., Fahrbach, K., et al. (2004, October 13). Bariatric surgery: a systematic review and meta-analysis. *Journal of the American Medical Association, 292*(14), 1724–1737.

DeMaria, E. J. (2007, May 24). Bariatric surgery for morbid obesity. *New England Journal of Medicine, 356*(21), 2176–2183.

Eating Disorders Coalition. (n.d.). Retrieved January 11, 2008, from http://www.eatingdisorderscoalition.org.

Epigee Women's Health. (n.d.). Retrieved January 11, 2008, from http://www.epigee.org/pregnancy/drugs/.

Food Allergy and Anaphylaxis Network. (n.d.). Retrieved January 12, 2008, from http://www.foodallergy.org.

Guthman, J. (2008, January–February). The food police: Why Michael Pollan makes me want to eat Cheetos. *Utne Reader, 145,* 44–47.

Hellmich, N. (2006, April 5). Athletes' hunger to win fuels eating disorders. *USA Today* online. Retrieved January 12, 2008, from http://www.usatoday.com/news/health/default.htm.

Kearney-Cooke, A., & Ackard, D. (1999, November–December). Far-reaching effects of sexual abuse. *Eating Disorders Today, 10,* 6.

Kolata, G. (2007). *Rethinking thin: The new science of weight loss—and the myths and realities of dieting.* New York: Farrar, Straus and Giroux.

Martin, C. (2008, January–February). Love your fat self: Rejecting fear, loathing and sacrifice. *Utne Reader, 145,* 38–43.

Mayo Clinic online. (n.d.). Retrieved January 11, 2008, from http://www.mayo clinic.com.

MedicineNet. (n.d.). Retrieved January 10, 2008, from http://www.medicinenet.com.

MedScape. (n.d.). Retrieved January 11, 2008, from http://www.medscape.com.

Metabolic Syndrome Institute. (n.d.). Retrieved January 11, 2008, from http://www.-metabolic-syndrome-institute.org.

Mickley, D. (2004, Summer). Medication for anorexia nervosa and bulimia nervosa. *Eating Disorders Today, 2*(4), 1.

Multi-service Eating Disorders Association (formerly Massachusetts Eating Disorders Association). (n.d.). Retrieved December 13, 2007, and January 10, 11, 12, 2008, from http://www.medainc.org/.

National Center for Health Statistics. (n.d.). Retrieved January 12, 2008, from http://www.ced.gov/nchs/data/.

National Eating Disorders Association. (n.d.). Retrieved January 11 and 12, 2008, from http://www.nationaleatingdisorders.org.

Nestle, M. (2006). *What to eat.* New York: North Point Press.

Reindl, S. (2001). *Sensing the self: Women's recovery from bulimia.* Cambridge, MA: Harvard University Press.

Sleep Disorders Guide. (n.d.). Retrieved January 12, 2008, from http://www.sleepdis-ordersguide.com.

Sports Coach Brian Mac. (n.d.). Retrieved January 11, 2008, from http://www.brian-mac.co.uk.

Stein, R. (2007, August 23). Weight loss surgery tied to a longer life. Retrieved January 12, 2008, from http://www.washingtonpost.com.

Szep, J. (2007, February 1). Binge eating is major health problem: study. Retrieved January 12, 2008, from http://www.scientificamerican.com.

Tsao, A. (2004, October 28). Weighing bariatric surgery risks. Retrieved January 10, 2008, from http://www.businessweek.com.

Turner, S., Hamilton, H., Jacobs, M., Angood, L., & Dwyer, D. (1997). The influence of fashion magazines on the body image satisfaction of college women: An exploratory analysis. *Adolescence, 32*(127), 603–614.

U.S. Department of Agriculture. (n.d.). Retrieved January 11, 2008, from http://www.mypyramid.gov.

U.S. Department of Health and Human Services. (n.d.). Retrieved January 11, 2008, from http://www.surgeongeneral.gov/.

WebMD. (n.d.). Retrieved January 11 and 12, 2008, from http://www.webmd.com.

Wonderlich, S., Crosby, R., Mitchell, J., Roberts, J., Haseltine, B., DeMuth, G., et al. (2000). Relationship of childhood sexual abuse and eating disturbance in children. *Journal of the American Academy of Children and Adolescent Psychiatry, 39*(10), 1277–1283.

Index